How to Read and Pray
THE PASSION STORY

Marilyn Gustin

D1051729

LIGUORI
PUBLICATIONS

One Liguori Drive
Liguori, MO 63057-9999
(314) 464-2500

Imprimi Potest:
James Shea, C.SS.R.
Provincial, St. Louis Province
The Redemptorists

Imprimatur:
+ Edward J. O'Donnell, D.D.
Archdiocesan Administrator, Archdiocese of St. Louis

ISBN 0-89243-590-9
Library of Congress Catalog Card Number: 93-78615

Scripture used in this text is taken from the NEW AMERICAN BIBLE
WITH REVISED NEW TESTAMENT, Copyright © 1986, AND REVISED
PSALMS, Copyright © 1991, by the Confraternity of Christian
Doctrine, 3211 Fourth Street, N.E., Washington, D.C. Used with
permission. All rights reserved.

Clip Art of the Christian World, copyright © 1984 by The Order of
St. Benedict, Inc. Published by The Liturgical Press, Collegeville,
Minnesota. Used with permission.

Cover design by Myra Buechting
Photo credit: Comstock, Inc.

Contents

Acknowledgments

In writing this book, I was greatly indebted to *The Passion Series* by Father Donald Senior, C.P., Professor of New Testament at Catholic Theological Union. Also, my continuing thanks goes to Father Raymond E. Brown, S.S., retired Professor of Scripture at Union Theological Seminary.

Introduction

Of all the stories about Jesus, the account of his passion and death is probably the most familiar to everyone, with the possible exception of the Christmas story. Jesus' suffering and crucifixion have been central to Christian reflection, devotion, and theology since the earliest days of Christianity. Had not his disciples experienced the resurrection of Jesus so powerfully, of course, the passion might have been forgotten. Nevertheless, the crucifixion has been understood as the source of Jesus' gift to all his followers.

Yet as much as we already know about the passion, we may never have considered the precise details of the gospel accounts. We may never have reflected deeply on the events that led up to Jesus' last days on earth. Some people have prayed the Stations of the Cross all their lives without ever having opened the Bible to read the "real" story.

How to Read and Pray the Passion Story invites you to study the scriptural portrayals of Jesus during his passion and crucifixion, of the other people involved, and of the surrounding events. Of course, this book provides only a beginning for study; many large volumes would be required to exhaust the subject. Perhaps it is inexhaustible!

As you read this book, you will be invited to reflect on and pray about this subject and to deepen your capacity to receive the grace of Christ by meditating on his suffering and death. To this end, biblical references are included. I recommend that you read this book with a Bible in hand and perhaps several bookmarks as well. That way, you can follow events in the sequence in which the gospel writers describe them. In this way, your study will be servant to your prayer.

Prayer, of course, cannot be done *by* the book in the same way that study can be offered in print. Prayer must occur in your own heart and mind. The suggestions given here are merely springboards for your own exploration and practice. If you just read this book, you will doubtless gain something. But your effort will produce fruit a hundredfold if you pray deeply over what you are studying.

The *Rule* of Saint Benedict, which has guided thousands of people toward a deeper life with God, strongly advised a life of balance between prayer (the first priority), work, and study. Everyone was to engage regularly in all three activities. The three-point balance provides a strong foundation for Christian spiritual growth.

How to Read and Pray the Passion Story provides study materials and suggestions for prayer. (Work is left to you!) Try to spend equal time with study and with prayer. Using the book as a Lenten exercise, either alone or with a group, provides a wonderful opportunity to establish a *lasting* practice of regular prayer and study. If you do so (especially if you haven't been so regular with prayer and study up to now), your spiritual life will soar.

CHAPTER ONE

Gospel Background of the Passion

The story of Jesus' suffering is recounted in each of the four gospels. Mark, Matthew, and Luke tell it in similar ways but with individual emphases. John tells a story in some ways quite different from that of the first three gospels (called the Synoptic Gospels because they are so similar. *Synoptic* means "seen together"). To understand the reasons for the differences, we need to recall what a "gospel" is—and what it is not.

If we think that the gospels are intended as objective, neutral reports of the events of Jesus' life and of the words he spoke, we will certainly misunderstand their depth and the splendid message each one wants to offer the reader. A gospel recounts memories and understandings held dear in the earliest Christian communities—memories of Jesus' life, death, and teaching. But none of them was written down until at least thirty-five years after Jesus' physical departure from the earth. The last one—John—was not completed until some time in the A.D. 90s.

During those decades, Christians not only remembered, they reflected, pondered, and asked questions about the meaning of it all. They projected certain parts of their experience and certain understandings won only by long meditation backward into the life of Jesus, telling them as if they had been there from the beginning.

Biblical scholars have worked hard to discover the earliest memories, the "message" emphases, and all the projections present in the gospel stories of Jesus. No one knows for sure how all the details fit historically. Factual discrepancies among the four gospels remain. It is precisely those differences, however, that yield some of our best insights and offer deeper understandings.

A gospel, then, is a composition of memories, reflections, understandings, messages, and convictions centering around Jesus, his life, his death and resurrection, and his teachings. Together, the four gospels are rather like a conglomerate portrait—one that seeks to be truthful to the inner meaning of Jesus and to be faithful to Christian memory and experience. It cannot have been an easy task to write a gospel, nor is it an easy task to fully understand the gospels.

The passion story is an integral part of each gospel. In each telling, the passion emphasizes the interests of the whole of the gospel to which it belongs. In each one, the passion is the climax of the gospel and grows out of the writer's understanding of previous events as well as of the passion itself. For these reasons, it is important to know a little about each gospel before looking at the passion stories themselves.

The Gospel of Mark

The Gospel of Mark was the first one to be written. It has been dated by scholars to the A.D. 60s, some thirty years after

Jesus. No one knows who the author was. People of that time were simply not as interested in such questions as we are, so they did not say. Some commentators over the centuries have thought that the author of Mark was close to Peter in his last years. No evidence to prove or disprove this theory is available, however.

What we can gather from the contents of Mark's gospel is that it has an atmosphere of impending doom—which might be related to the passion (after all, everyone knew the end of the story) but might also be related to the situation of the writer.

Because there are Latin words in the original Greek text, it is generally thought that Mark was written in Italy, probably in Rome. If so, the situation of Christians was precarious because the Roman emperor Nero was so cruelly unpredictable. He blamed the great fire of Rome in this decade on the Christians, and they suffered for it. Although they were not subjected to a full-scale official persecution, the lives of Christians must have seemed much less secure after that.

Moreover, many Christians in Rome were Jewish. The Jews "back home" in Palestine were once again in revolution against Rome. Jews everywhere must have been unsettled by the war, although the outcome was not complete until A.D. 70, the year Jerusalem was successfully besieged by Titus, son of the new emperor, Vespasian. The Temple was leveled and burned, never to be rebuilt. (The Western Wall in modern Jerusalem is the foundation of the ancient Temple, the only remaining stones of that magnificent place of worship.) Since the Temple seems to be still standing in Mark's Gospel, it is dated to the late 60s.

Mark can be said to have three main interests that make his gospel a bit different (at least in emphasis) from those of Matthew or Luke. Although all three pass along Jesus' central teaching about the kingdom or reign of God, Mark treats Jesus' life almost as a parable of the kingdom. For Mark, everything Jesus did—especially his miracles and the passion/resurrection—pointed to the kingdom and its meaning.

Mark is also interested in what scholars have called the "messianic secret." More so than in the other gospels, Mark's Jesus repeatedly tells his disciples and others not to speak of him as Messiah. In fact, Jesus himself seems not to be happy with this title. Of course, the term *messiah* had heavy political implications, so perhaps Mark downplayed this title for Jesus—though he does use it—because he was unwilling to set Christians at risk.

Mark also gives us a great deal of information about the disciples and what it means to be a disciple. More than in the other gospels, Jesus' disciples in Mark misunderstand and don't "get it" for a long time. In fact, the situation seems to worsen during the passion. The disciples fail miserably in Mark.

These main themes are presented in such a way that the passion grows out of them. The way Jesus lived made conflict with religious and political leaders inevitable. Thus, Mark regards the suffering of Jesus as an essential part of his mission, organically connected to everything that came before it.

The Gospel of Matthew

Since Matthew demonstrably used Mark as one of his sources of information, we know that The Gospel of Matthew was written later. Most modern scholars place it in the A.D. 80s because the historical situation of that period fits. The Jews no longer have a Temple, and they are, of necessity, beginning to be more exclusive about Judaism. Matthew seems to react to this situation at times. More precise dating than that is debatable.

The writer of Matthew, like the author of The Gospel of Mark, is unknown. He was clearly a leader in some Christian community—not in Palestine proper—and some have speculated that he may have lived in Antioch in Syria. He seems to have been Jewish in background. Some scholars regard his familiarity with the Hebrew Scriptures (our Old Testament) as evidence that he had been a rabbi, that is, trained in the Jewish Law.

The community for which Matthew wrote, however, was clearly a mixed community with both Jewish and gentile interests. The very first Christians were Jews. Later, after the destruction of the Temple, it became necessary for the preservation of Jewish identity to exclude Christians from the synagogue. Matthew's gospel seems to have been written after this. It may have been, in part, an attempt to redefine the place of Jewish Christians in relationship to their own background as well as the place of Gentiles in the community.

There are some very harsh words in Matthew against Jewish leadership. The intensity may or may not have been Jesus' own but does reflect the feelings of Jewish Christians no longer allowed to participate in Jewish life. However, in no way can these words be interpreted as being directed against Jews as a whole—not then, not now. We must remember that Jewish Christians and Jewish Jews had much to disagree about, and like most family arguments, this one got bitter.

Matthew emphasizes Jesus' teaching more than his miracles, in some contrast to Mark. Matthew presents Jesus as a continuation and fulfillment of the Hebrew Scriptures and organizes Jesus' teachings in a way that reflects the connections. Such themes as "the Law and the Prophets" and their fulfillment and the typically Jewish emphasis on right living are both prominent in Matthew.

Matthew uses the Hebrew Scriptures constantly, sometimes quoting them directly, sometimes referring to them almost automatically. These references were immediately recognizable to his early audience and to modern people who have studied the Old Testament.

Matthew thinks of the Church as already organized, largely along Old Testament patterns. He knows it has a world mission and writes that Jesus commissioned its work. The Church, as Matthew sees it, is the "people of God" in his own time, as the Israelites were the people of God in previous centuries.

In Matthew, the passion haunts the whole book. From the beginning in the stories around his birth, reaction to Jesus is sharply divided. Some people, like the gentile magi, worship him wholeheartedly; others, like Herod, who killed the babies of Bethlehem, are ready to destroy him. So right from the start, we see Jesus rejected and death coming because of him. However, an ultimate victory is equally foreshadowed. Herod's efforts fail, and Jesus arrives safely in Galilee, for example.

The passion grows out of a huge shift that Matthew perceives between the time of the Old Covenant and the time of the New Covenant in Christ. Death is inevitable in such a transition. Jesus' death is inevitable as a direct outgrowth of his leading this transition. Every setback, however, be it a small argument or Jesus' death itself, becomes in Matthew an opportunity for God to create the new life and the new people he intends. For Matthew also, then, the passion is fully integrated with Jesus' whole life and closely related to his ministry and teaching.

The Gospel of Luke

The earliest traditions of the Christian community suggest that the writer of The Gospel of Luke was a physician who may have been a companion of Paul (although there are some problems with this theory). The gospel is the first part of a two-part work, the second part being The Acts of the Apostles. Wherever Luke came from, he clearly did not know Palestine firsthand because his geography is sometimes inaccurate. Just where he did come from, however, is still much debated.

Luke, like Matthew, uses Mark's gospel as a source. Luke and Matthew also contain some material from a common source modern scholars call "Q" (from the German *Quelle*, source) that does not appear in Mark. Luke and Matthew each used unique sources as well.

Luke, for historical reasons similar to those affecting Matthew, is thought to have been written also in the A.D. 80s. Luke's gospel differs from Matthew's, however, in that it is written in fine Greek and shows evidence of the conscious use of Greek literary forms—indicating a well-educated, non-Jewish background for the writer.

Luke writes for an almost entirely gentile Christian community. While he does not show the interest in Jewish concerns that appears in Matthew, he does want to clarify the position of gentile Christians in relation to the roots of their faith in Judaism. Luke does not want to bind gentile Christians to the old Law but insists that believers in Jesus inherit the promises of God through the Old Covenant. Luke gives particular attention to the place of the downtrodden within the Christian house. Luke-Acts shows no evidence of actual persecution of Christians but rather considerable vexation from Jewish leaders, neighbors, and even family members.

Luke emphasizes Jesus' concern for society's "little people," including women as well as social outcasts. Many of the details in his stories highlight the gentleness of Jesus and the power of his healing heart. For Luke, Jesus is a prophet rejected by his people's leaders but profoundly supported by God in an offer of divine mercy to all.

The passion in Luke-Acts is subordinated somewhat to the resurrection and the power of the Holy Spirit in the fledgling Christian community. Of course, the resurrection comes *after* the passion and is dependent on it. Luke knows this and understands that the passion is itself of immense value. Yet The Gospel of Luke differs from those of Matthew and Mark in that it does not stand so much under the shadow of the passion. Jesus is a little different, even during the passion, in Luke than he is in Mark and Matthew.

The Gospel of John

As already mentioned, John has an altogether different flavor than the Synoptic Gospels. John's chronology and arrangement of the material are also different. He includes long speeches or discourses, purportedly by Jesus yet unclear in their boundaries, which explain the significance of much of Jesus' teaching. Through the centuries, it has been the favorite gospel of many mystical saints because of its obvious interest in Jesus' oneness with the Father and the extension of this same possibility to believers.

The factualness of John has been much debated over the centuries, seemingly going in and out of scholarly favor. Some scholars think the Synoptics have a better grasp of the history of Jesus, but others have recently pointed out that John is the only gospel with even a secondhand claim to eyewitness reports. (See John 21:24.) Consequently, many historical questions cannot be finally answered.

The Gospel of John stems from the "Johannine community," a group of churches originally in Judea and Samaria. It reflects the interests as well as prejudices and difficulties of these churches. Included in these prejudices and difficulties is the strong language against the "Jews," which without exception means the Jewish leadership who opposed Jesus. This gospel writer knew that the leadership would expel Christians from the synagogue. This did not happen historically until at least the A.D. 80s, however, so the date of the final editing of John is usually placed in the early A.D. 90s.

The purpose of John's gospel is to encourage "belief" in Jesus—but a belief that is far more than assent to a list of rational propositions. Belief is the whole, trustful, totally open, relationship between Jesus and a disciple—a transforming relationship culminating in union with the Father and with the Son in eternal life.

The Gospel of John is organized into four parts. The Prologue (1:1-18) introduces the main themes of the gospel. The Book of Signs (1:10–12:50) portrays Jesus' ministry and focuses on the coming "hour" when Jesus will be glorified. The third division, The Book of Glory (13:1–20:31), begins with the Last Supper and describes Jesus'passion, death, and resurrection. The Epilogue: The Resurrection Appearance in Galilee (Chapter 21) continues the account of Jesus' post-Resurrection appearances to his disciples. Here, too, we find discourses of great depth and beauty, especially about the disciples' relationship with Jesus.

In John's Gospel, the passion is the ultimate goal of Jesus' whole life. Here, there is no victimization. Jesus is the orchestrator of all the events of the passion, for the Father has turned over to Jesus all the power there is. For John, the passion-resurrection-Spirit is one grand triumph: the glorification of the Son. And this glorification, coupled with profound belief in Jesus Christ, enables the disciple to become literally a "child of God."

Stories as Theology and Spiritual Instruction

Nowhere in the Synoptics, and only in the Prologue of John, can we find anything close to propositions about who Jesus was or what the goal of discipleship is. Instead, the gospel writers tell the story of Jesus. Each one tells it masterfully to *show* who Jesus was and to instruct the disciple, either by example or by brief comment. The exception to this pattern is, of course, the long discourses in John. But even there, the teaching is placed in a story context—though the discourses often burst the boundaries of the story and go somewhere else.

In the gospels, the story is an expression of understanding and a powerful effort to draw the reader actively into the story, to participate in the transformation of the disciples.

One reason for this narrative approach is that we remember stories rather easily. The stories are dear to our hearts. In fact, because of the stories, our hearts may understand more than our minds can express in words. It is to stories, in all parts of our life, that we return again and again. Every family has favorite stories, told and retold at every get-together. Every individual has a fund of stories he or she loves to tell over and over again. Every public speaker knows that if the audience begins to drift away, a reliable attention-getter is "once upon a time." Stories are powerful in themselves. Jesus' life, ministry, and passion took place day to day like any other life. The gospel stories are powerful expressions of the meaning of his life.

Throughout Scripture there are levels of understanding and interpretation. One level is always the historical. Jesus *did* live, and much of what is remembered and recounted in the gospels is factual. Sometimes, however, the purported facts do not agree from gospel to gospel. And no evidence is available to settle the questions.

However, the deeper significance of the stories is their *meaning*. We can understand fact, then, as one level of scriptural truth and *meaning* as another more profound level of truth.

The attempt to resolve factual discrepancies is a fascinating effort, but it does not engage us at the deepest spiritual level of our own being. Meaning—the meaning of the stories as we have them—does. It is at the level of meaning that we understand Jesus—his life, his purposes, his splendor. Meaning in the gospels tells us what discipleship is about and how we may be fulfilled in it. Meaning in Scripture instructs us about the ways we can live and find the glorious life that the gospels offer us.

Facts are interesting, and the big facts ground the gospel stories. Meanings are life-transforming when taken fully into the heart. Meanings are the purpose of this study of the passion. Meanings are best gleaned from stories. Then they unfold organically instead of being merely dry explanations.

The Passion and Our Hearts

Meister Eckhart said that the birth of Jesus happens continuously, but it can do us no good at all until he is born in our hearts. A similar truth belongs to the passion. Jesus' passion occurred in a particular time and place, but it does us no good until his death occurs in our own hearts, our own spirits. Whatever the passion and death of Jesus means, it is useless to us unless that meaning is fully assimilated in our innermost being.

That cannot happen merely from reading (or writing) a book. But a book can point to meanings and suggest possibilities for action (including prayer) so you can assimilate the passion of the Lord—perhaps more deeply than you have yet done. That is the intention of this writing.

The passion story describes what happened to Jesus. But it

also portrays what must happen to us if we would share in the spiritual transformation his death makes available. Resurrection occurred externally, perceivably, in Jesus. Spiritual resurrection (or transformation) must occur inwardly in us and must then become perceivable through our living. So as we examine the passion of Jesus, we will be looking especially for helps for our own spiritual assimilation of Jesus' death and all that went along with it. What we learn by praying with the events of the passion of Jesus—with its external occurrences—tells us a great deal about what will be happening within our own being if we are committed disciples.

To help us focus on this purpose, consider the familiar statement of Jesus in Luke 9:23: "If anyone wishes to come after me, he must deny himself and take up his cross daily and follow me." Perhaps you have assumed that you know what that statement means. Yet you can probably deepen your present understanding. The question that guides your study and your prayer throughout this book, then, will be, "What does it mean *spiritually* to deny myself and take up my cross and follow Jesus?"

Two Beginning Methods of Prayer

Rather than repeat the same instructions several times, I am presenting here two basic types of prayer you can use when praying with the passion stories—or any other part of Scripture.

Lectio Divina

For centuries, "divine reading" (that's what *lectio divina* means in Latin) has been a familiar and beloved way of praying with Scripture. The process has been well described by ancient and modern Christian writers. Details vary, but the basic pattern is as follows.

1. Decide where your reading will begin, and mark the place.

2. Go to a spot where you can be alone, uninterrupted and quiet for a predetermined period of time. It can be fifteen minutes; it can be an hour or more. It's up to you. But turn off everything, including the phone, and shut whatever doors you must. This is your own time with God and with the Bible.

3. Make yourself physically comfortable. Not so comfortable that you fall asleep but comfortable enough to relax so your body will not distract you from your focus on the Scripture. Often taking several slow, deep breaths will help you calm down.

4. Open your Bible to the marked place and begin to read. In earlier times, reading was always aloud, and this is still a powerful practice. But silent reading is good, too. More important is that your reading be *slow*. This is not the time to "get through" a chapter. You have marked where you wish to begin. It doesn't matter where you stop, even if it's after only a single phrase!

5. Read until a word, a phrase, or an idea strikes your heart or catches your attention. Stop at that point. Repeat the meaningful phrase to yourself over and over. You may think aloud about what it means to you if you wish, but the simple repetition may be more vital. Repetition will help you take the phrase into your heart of hearts—where your attention was first piqued. Just allow yourself gently to live with the phrase until it seems to be complete or no longer draws you.

Then move along to the next words, reading again until another point strikes you as special. Repeat the process as often as you wish, for as long as you have time.

6. If this reading leads you into direct prayer, addressing God or Jesus or the Spirit directly, so much the better. That's the real intent of the reading. Don't glue yourself to the book

if your heart wants to go to God! Going to God is the reason not only for this careful reading but for the whole of Christianity. So even the smallest opportunity should be eagerly followed.

7. When your time is up, or when your heart seems filled for the moment, be sure to give God thanks—thanks for the Bible, thanks for the prayer, thanks for the time with him, thanks for whatever has just happened in your *lectio divina*.

8. Then gently, keeping the "feel" of the prayer and reading as much as you can, go about your life.

Some people like to keep a journal of their *lectio divina*, to write down particular insights or experiences or even to record what they have read. This is not necessary, but you may wish to experiment with it and discover for yourself if it helps you. Some people find it immensely enriching; others find it merely a distraction. Only you can decide.

Personalizing the Scene

Prayer takes many forms. The aim of all forms of prayer is to "bring" us closer to the Lord. We don't have to be concerned about bringing the Lord closer to us; he is already nearer than we even imagine. But we are so often far from him, far in our thoughts, in our emotional involvements with everyday matters, even in our dreams and hopes and worries (*especially* in our worries, we are far from him).

So whatever prayer will bring us more into the Lord's company will be a genuine help to us. One form of prayer that many people have come to love was strongly advocated by Saint Ignatius of Loyola and is still taught in many retreats. In this prayer, one puts oneself imaginatively into the biblical scene and follows the events from the standpoint of an insider. Who of us has not wished to be physically with Jesus? Take that wish into this kind of prayer.

You may wish to add yourself to those who are already in the scene. In the passion scenes, you might be a bystander, a soldier, one of the Sanhedrin, an unnamed disciple in Jesus' company. Or you might wish to identify yourself with one of the known characters. You might become Peter or one of the other disciples; you might be the woman who anoints Jesus just before the passion or the maid in the courtyard of the high priest. You might even become Jesus!

However you get into the scene, respond freely to your own experience once you are there. Be there in the confusion of the arrest. Do you also run away? Let yourself admire the way Jesus handles himself in one situation or another. Consider how you would feel, think, or act if you were in his place. Maybe you want to "get inside" Judas, or perhaps you have betrayed a loved one and want to live with Peter for a while.

Whatever your spontaneous imaginative experience, allow it to be. Do not evaluate it or refuse any feeling or thought that may come up. Be as fully into the events as you are able.

When you are ready to come back to your ordinary personal viewpoint, take time to ponder the meaning of what you have experienced. Sometimes you may find your appreciation of Jesus and your love for him expanded and deepened. Sometimes you may be startled at what your emotions or your actions in the imagined scene tell you about yourself.

For example, I once received the insight in this form of prayer that I departed before every scene was over. I was always the first one to leave. How odd, I thought. Looking a little deeper, I saw that it happened when I didn't have anything more to say or didn't know what more to do. I left. You miss a lot of punch lines when you do that in real life! And you miss moments of unstructured being together with other people. And, if you are like me, you also get nervous when you don't have any action to take (control to exercise) in the next moment.

This awareness made me uncomfortable, though it hardly seemed a serious sin. But it meant that when I feel God has withdrawn, the chances are better than a thousand to one that *I* have departed from God and have thereby not received what was available in God's gifts of presence.

This kind of prayer—being in the scene and pondering it afterward—gave me a new insight about a next step in growth toward full awareness of the Lord's presence. It was as if the Lord said, "Look at this. What would you like to do about it?" It continued the ever increasing awareness of dialogue with God that a steady habit of prayer offers.

Using This Book

This book may be used by individuals, families, or other groups. It is designed to be used alongside the Bible, not by itself. In order to understand what is written, you will want to follow along in the suggested biblical readings. Most of them are familiar, but you are encouraged to try to read them fresh— as if you had never seen them before.

The book is designed to help you grow from your study and prayer. It is not intended to be academic, although insights from scholars are included where useful. Every reflection aims to help you reflect on your own experience and your own living, to assist you in making choices that will deepen your awareness of God and bring you closer to him.

The main part of the book, Chapters Two and Three, are organized around the individual scenes of the passion stories in the gospels. In each section, you will be given readings, suggestions, and questions for your own pondering with added reflections to help you explore areas you may not have thought of.

To help you compare and reflect on the implications of the passion story in all four gospels, an appendix is provided, beginning on page 107. Here you will find biblical references and questions and comments to further aid you in "breaking open" the passion story.

This book is like a table full of food with a number of dishes offered. If you like to read a book straight through without interruption, this one may seem to have big gaps in it. It is a book to help you ponder Scripture and pray with the Word of God. Each section has a natural pattern of its own, and none is very long. You may study one section at a time, if you wish, or more than one if you have larger blocks of times available. But don't "overeat" at this table—it will do you no good.

Because of the subject, you might feel especially drawn to *How to Read and Pray the Passion Story* during Lent. The passion is for our whole Christian life, however, and this book can intensify your awareness of its place in your life at any season. This book could be a Lenten study for individuals or groups, or it could be the backbone of a private or group retreat at any time. It could be a book to be picked up for evening quiet or morning prayer along with the Bible.

Whichever way you choose to use this book, take your time with it. Your own active participation is at least half of its value.

CHAPTER TWO

The Passion in Matthew, Mark, and Luke

In each of the Synoptic Gospels, the reader is fully prepared for the passion and death of Jesus long before the events are described. Similarly, each community/audience knew the end of the story before it began. The suffering, death, and resurrection of Jesus were the main sources of reflection for the earliest Christians. It was here they found their most intense questions and also here that they—especially those who had not known Jesus physically—experienced the beginnings of profound devotion to the Lord.

It was for them, and us as well, a little like what happens when you know the end of an exciting detective movie. Your interest is not in finding out what happened but in seeing *how* it happened and what it meant. The gospels are not suspense thrillers; everyone already knows the outcome. But how did it happen? Why did it happen? What meaning can we draw from the events and the teachings embedded in them?

The Conspiracy Against Jesus

Throughout all their pages, the three Synoptic Gospels point to Jesus' death. Therefore, when the conspiracy against Jesus becomes active enough to be "announced," it comes as no surprise. It is merely what we readers have been expecting all along. A statement that the leaders are actively trying to find a way to arrest and kill Jesus opens the passion accounts in Matthew 26:1-5, Mark 14:1-2, and Luke 22:1-2.

In each account, the leaders of the religious establishment are cautious and reluctant to attack Jesus openly. In Matthew and Mark, they don't want to act during festival time when huge crowds of pilgrims came to Jerusalem. These crowds were already inclined to be volatile—as the Romans acknowledged by strengthening their contingent of soldiers during every festival. The leaders didn't want to light any uncontrollable fires! Luke says only that the leaders were afraid of the people —and so they seemed to be.

In all three gospels, Judas provides the opportunity the leaders were seeking. They would have waited in their caution, but here was one of Jesus' inner circle who was willing to help them. (See Matthew 26:14-16, Mark 14:10-11, and Luke 22:3-6.) In Matthew, Judas' motive is money—he asks for it. In Mark, Judas simply offers his services, though he will be rewarded. In Luke, Judas' motivation is that "Satan entered into him."

So now, before the Last Supper, every reader knows that Judas is awaiting the opportune moment.

Judas' action is made especially bitter in Matthew and Mark by the contrast with the woman who anointed Jesus while he was eating (Matthew 26:6-13 and Mark 14:3-9). In these gospels, rejection of the Lord is often placed side by side with highest appreciation of Jesus. The theme of opposite responses continues here. It is as if Matthew and Mark are saying to us readers, "The conspiracy is on! Everything is in place for Jesus to suffer and to die. Which way do you respond to it?"

Since you are reading this book, you have already "chosen sides" at some level or other. No one would deliberately side with Judas, even if active discipleship were not in question. But do not hurry past this opposition and its implications. If you have not actively rejected Jesus and the possibilities he offers, have you done anything as fine as the *active* gift of the anonymous woman?

For Your Reflection

One way to reflect on this question is to think of Judas at one end of a continuum and the woman's pure love at the other end. Where do you stand right now on that continuum? Jesus' disciples at the table were irritated at the woman. She could have fed the poor with all that expensive perfume! From what motivation are your gifts given to the Lord?

Jesus' famous response (look again at the stories) is not a suggestion that the poor be ignored. Rather, Jesus is looking at the purity of the woman's love for him and the simplicity of her expression of it. He takes it as preparation of his body for burial (a sacred duty in Judaism), but he points beyond that, too: "She has done a good thing for me."

The woman's act is direct, heartfelt, spontaneous, full of love. When have you acted in that immediate, loving way? You may not have had the physical body of Jesus to anoint, but "whatever you did for one of these least brothers of mine, you did for me" (Matthew 25:40). When have you looked for the beauty in someone and then responded wholeheartedly and without worrying about the cost in time or in money?

The woman's act is not a response to *need* in Jesus but to the goodness and beauty she loves in him. When have you done something "just for love" outside your own family or circle of friends? Surely, there is another hint here about what it means to follow Jesus through the passion, to deny oneself: the pure, spontaneous expressions of love and gratitude for someone who does not need us but whom we admire or love.

If you have never done something like this, put yourself in the woman's place as you reread the story. Let her teach you how. Then ask the Lord to help you be alert to opportunities—and to grace you with the purity to *act on love* the next chance you have.

I was once "one of these least" ones for such a pure act of love, and the experience altered something very deep in me. A nun, whose personal allowance (for toothpaste and everything) was less than fifty dollars a month, saved her dollars until she had enough to buy me a seventy-five-dollar gift. I learned later that I was not the first to be given her pure love in material form. Nor would I be the last. The sheer beauty of her purity still brings tears to my eyes.

May we follow the example of such women! It may tell us more about the cross than we imagine.

The Last Supper and the Argument

With the conspiracy now well under way, the reader knows that Jesus is in mortal danger. Jesus knows it, too, for he foretold it before the events of the passion stories occurred. The disciples are not yet clear about what is going on. In this atmosphere, Jesus sends them to prepare the Passover meal.

At the table, in all three of the Synoptics, three events occur: Jesus makes a New Covenant with his disciples, he announces that he will be betrayed by one of them, and he predicts Peter's denial of him. Read Matthew 26:17-35, Mark 14:12-31, Luke 22:7-38.

In Matthew and Mark, the announcement about betrayal comes first. But these gospels do not say that Judas departs. In these two stories, then, it may be assumed that Judas is present for the New Covenant, the Eucharist. He is included in spite of what Jesus knows about him.

This is one of the most stupendous acts of loving one's enemies that could be imagined, isn't it? Jesus expresses here the love that is God within him: he gives himself in covenant for those who will follow him and for those who will not, for those who will support him and those who will betray him. He gives himself for everyone—good and bad, follower and betrayer, believer and rejecter.

He gives himself for people of all times, because in "do[ing] this in memory of me," no one of any age needs to be excluded. He gives himself forever. Surely we, twenty centuries later and of very mixed character, can be utterly grateful that Jesus made his New Covenant for everyone who wants it.

This New Covenant is our whole relationship with Jesus Christ. But it is focused in the Eucharist, just as Jesus focused it in the sharing of the Passover bread, which he said was his own body, and the Passover cup of wine, which he said was his own blood "shed for many." In the biblical tradition, covenants were sealed in blood. So, too, was Jesus' New Covenant in the Eucharist.

In Luke, the announcement of the betrayal comes after the meal of the New Covenant, but the betrayer is not identified. In Luke, something quite different occurs. They start to discuss who among them could betray Jesus, and suddenly they are arguing about who among them is the greatest!

This is not the first time such an argument has arisen. Both

Mark 9:33-37 and Luke 9:46-48 report an earlier scrap over the same question. But how could it arise again in the context of the disciples' last meal with their Lord? Jesus had just given them himself, his whole being, in perpetual covenant sealed with his own blood—and what do they do? They become wrapped up in plain old egocentric questions: "Am I better than you? Or are you better than me?"

For Your Reflection

Before you say to yourself that you've never been in that kind of an argument, pause. You may not have battled out loud, in exact words, over "who is greatest." But reflect on the following questions.

- Do I compare myself to other people? What is the purpose of these comparisons? What is their result? Does one of us come out "better"? Then what happens to my own inner attitude?

- Have I ever argued over who is right about some issue or other? Is the interest of the ego the same as who is the greatest?

- Have I ever gotten into arguments right before or right after going to church? What does receiving the Eucharist then mean?

- When I reflect on my attitudes and habits of argument in light of Luke 22:25-27, what do I discover? How can I grow in the qualities Jesus suggests here?

You may wish to list a few possibilities for experiment. Here is one suggestion to help you begin. When you realize you are in the midst of a verbal argument or a mental comparison, stop. Simply stop. Close your mouth and distract yourself until you are in touch with whatever is actually going on. Then, if there *is* any issue that matters, you can return to the discussion—but from a genuine interest in serving the truth instead of winning the points.

A challenge? You bet! Worth it? It brings you closer to the heart of Christ. What do you think?

Are these also ways of taking up our own cross to follow the Lord?

The third event during the Last Supper is Jesus' prediction of Peter's denials. Peter, as we all know, cannot fathom that Jesus' words could be true. In this moment of intimate communion with his beloved Master, Peter is aware only of his love for Jesus—a love that has not yet been tested. As always, Peter is totally honest from his moment-to-moment awareness. But he cannot imagine that in a few hours the possibility of personal loss will threaten him so seriously that his love for Jesus is forgettable—not thrown away, just forgotten.

In Luke, Jesus' constant gentle care for people who are not yet transformed shows in his words to Peter. (See Luke 22:31-32.) Jesus knows that Peter is due for a big test, and he knows that Peter will fail. He gives him a commission for the future, however, because he also knows that Peter's weakness is forgivable and that Peter himself will be purified and will return.

This is so beautiful. Doesn't the Lord know us all in exactly this way? He knows our tendencies, and he will do whatever he can (which is a lot) to help us through the messes we create. Then, if we make a serious error, he will try to bring us back to himself and put us to work for him. I've often wondered how great a person Judas could have become if he had returned to Jesus and asked forgiveness instead of despairing. Forgiveness has phenomenal transforming power!

But even though the Lord knows what Peter will do, Peter still must go through it. Why? The answer comes at cockcrow, in Peter's response.

Uniquely in Luke 22:35-38, Jesus instructs his disciples to be prepared. He reminds them of the time he sent them out without material preparation but simply dependent on the bounty of God. Now, Jesus says, the times are different and preparedness is important. They understand that something threatening is coming, but they interpret it in a purely external way: they think their two swords will help. Jesus' words "It is enough" are enigmatic but do not seem to accept their response.

What the disciples miss is that Jesus speaks in figures of speech to try to prepare them inwardly for hard tests coming up. If this level of instruction was valuable for the Twelve on the night of Jesus' passion, how much more valuable it was for Luke's community of the 80s! This later generation of followers lived in a wholly uncertain legal situation and may well have expected persecution at any time. How good it must have been for them to hear that preparation was important, that they must be ready inside for hard tests and obstacles. We can only surmise their response, but within ten years came the first official persecution of Christians under the Emperor Diocletian. Perhaps Luke's warnings were well taken and followed.

And what about us twentieth-century folks? Legally, American Christians are protected. Whether or not we experience persecution as *Christians* may well depend on how thoroughly we live a recognizably Christian life. But legal or official challenge is not the only difficulty that truly Christian living can provoke.

Some people have thought that if we're not in disfavor with someone because of our Christianity, we're not strong enough Christians. Do you think that's true?

For Your Reflection

Give some thought to possible tests of your Christian commitment. Following the direction of Jesus' words and actions, how might you strengthen yourself for such tests?

Gethsemane, Arrest, and First Trial

After the New Covenant is made and the meal concluded, Jesus and his disciples go out to a place they have often gone before. It must have been a lovely spot. It is described as a garden. Its beauty must have been solace to the heart of Jesus as well as to his followers—who really did not know what was about to happen. The scene in Gethsemane is familiar. You may wish to reread it in each of the three gospels: Matthew 26:36-46, Mark 14:32-42, and Luke 22:39-46.

Let's look first at Jesus in this scene. He wants the support of his disciples. He keeps the three closest ones near him in this agonizing hour. In Matthew and Mark, he asks them to keep watch and pray, then later to pray that they not be put to the test. In Luke, they are to pray the same prayer. But they are not able to support him, so he is alone with God—except in Luke, where an angel comes to comfort him in his extreme pain.

It is impossible to get inside the psychology of Jesus. All we know for sure is that this time of prayer was extraordinarily intense and that his utter devotion to his Father's will won out over his own resistance to the coming suffering. The word *agony* is used only in Luke. It is a telling Greek term, *agonia*, but it does not mean simply intense pain. It comes from sports or combat and means an extraordinarily difficult but *victorious* struggle. Luke's readers would have known that. In the *agonia*, then, we see the victory of Jesus over his own not wanting to suffer or to die.

How did he win?

The too-familiar words "not what I will but what you will" both reveal and conceal the key. Because our smaller struggles often are the lens through which we see Jesus' struggle, we are inclined to take this phrase as expressing passive resignation. But from everything the gospels tell us about Jesus, resignation was not his way. His obedience to the Father was active and passionate. He took full initiative to act obediently.

In Gethsemane, Jesus admits his resistance, but far more intensely he *wants* the Father's will. He does not *want* his own way unless it is in full accord with what God wants. In this moment, I believe (though not everyone agrees) that Jesus was fully aware of his freedom to say "no" to the passion. He chose the will of God because that was what he wanted more than he wanted anything else, even his own safety.

How is it possible to be in that position inside one's own self? It must come from at least two inner qualities: total and unwavering love for God above *everything* else, including oneself, and total and unwavering conviction that God's will is the best and most beautiful direction for the whole universe and for every individual creature, including oneself.

How does one develop such glorious inner qualities? Not having them myself, I'm not sure. At the very least, they must involve constant practice with the smaller opportunities for loving God and obeying God's will in all the daily ways that arise in our lives. Jesus said that the person who is trustworthy in small things will be equally so in larger things. (See Luke 16:10.) So the small ways we love God and the small ways we obey when we understand God's will—those will be our foundation when greater love and greater obedience is required.

However Jesus' inner mind worked, he had won his own battle before the crowd arrived. The disciples, however, were, if anything, in worse shape by that time because they had been sleeping instead of praying. They simply couldn't face what was happening. Either they didn't fully believe it or understand it or they denied it in some way. In any case, Jesus' warnings and requests were ignored, and they could not stay awake. They were awakened by Jesus (again!) just before the crowd came to get him.

For Your Reflection

Is there anything to be learned in this scene about our own cross-carrying?

Consider the question. Then, before you read the next paragraph, make a list of your own insights. Did the disciples carry their crosses in this scene? How could they have done so? How does that carry over into your own life?

Here are two possibilities for your consideration. First, following Jesus in Gethsemane means willingness to face squarely into things, no matter how threatening or sorrowful they are. Ask yourself

- Do I look honestly, with clear sight and willing heart, at every circumstance—even those that show me to be less than I wish I were?

- Am I willing to see the truth in all situations, no matter the cost to myself?

- Do I sincerely *want* to obey God, or do I wish I wanted to?

- Do I depend on God totally and pray intensely about things that are rough or challenging or frightening?

- Do I seek courage and strength from God for whatever is coming, or do I only seek a way out of the difficulty? Just where do I stand? Would I rather sleep with the disciples or stay awake with Jesus?

Your answer in prayerful reflection now may not be the same as your past assumptions or your past behavior. Be ready to believe in your new answer and to act on it.

The second point for reflection on cross-carrying is *Wake up!* The notion of being fully awake is a deep one in spiritual life. At this deeper level, we are being called to full awareness of God in every moment. Being awake does not refer to our usual daily state of getting around. In spiritual terms, our daily life includes a great deal of sleep, that is, unconscious or automatic living.

We are not usually totally present to what is happening *right now*. If we were, we would also be totally aware of God's presence, because he is never absent. Instead, we attend to countless lesser matters and are asleep to God's life in us, to his love constantly offered to us.

When Jesus says "Wake up!" he calls us to full wakefulness to God, now and always.

Do we want it?

The Arrest

For the arrest scene, read Matthew 26:47-56, Mark 14:43-50, and Luke 22:47-53. The scene is easily understood.

Notice how Jesus treats Judas with gentle respect. In no way does he refuse the kiss of betrayal—which in other days might have been the kiss of friendship. Nor does he object to Judas' intention. In Matthew, he calls Judas "friend." In Luke, he lets Judas know that he knows what is happening. But all is done with dignity. Jesus accords to Judas the honorable treatment he offers without prejudice to all people.

The disciples react with violence to protect their Master. In Mark, Jesus ignores the gesture. In Matthew, he uses the moment to teach the disciples, refuses all help by implication, and affirms the fulfillment of Scripture. In Luke, he rebukes the violent act and heals the injured enemy. In each of these pictures of Jesus, we see a quality consistent with his portrayal in that particular gospel. In Mark, the event almost swirls around Jesus, while he himself is barely active. In Matthew, he is ever the teacher—and he demonstrates his own principles for living. In Luke, it is the compassionate healer who stands before Judas and the crowd.

So Jesus not only treats his enemies with respect, he takes initiative to help them as well, insofar as they are willing to receive healing.

For Your Reflection

If we follow Jesus daily, moving quietly under our own cross, what does the scene of Jesus' arrest suggest? How can we learn to treat all people with respect, no matter what their apparent worth and no matter what their attitudes toward us?

In a Scripture class years ago, we had a heated discussion about our attitude toward a man who had raped a teenager and then cut off both her lower arms. None of us knew him personally and had only seen the young woman on TV. The outrage in people's hearts was palpable in the room. How would Jesus have treated this man? Does his example with Judas show us the direction of his attitude?

The class finally concluded, with great emotion, that Jesus would treat all people with respect, condemning the act but extending love and dignity to the person. We ourselves cannot do such a thing simply by decision—especially if the circumstances are extreme. If we want to see and respond to the beauty in every human being as Jesus did, it will cost us.

We must practice. We must begin with those nearest us. Who are the people who most often receive lack of simple respect from our temper or our too-quick judgments? We begin there. We look for the image of God in the person and respond to *that*. We begin to treat the person as we would treat the Lord, for God is absent from no heart—though often ignored or denied.

Pause now and list a few ways in which you, in your ordinary relationships, might behave with more respect to those around you. Then choose one person and treat him or her better. Do it as an experiment but thoroughly and honestly, praying all the way for God's grace to help you. He will.

Second, Jesus gives an example in this incident of how we can be steady in our good purposes. He could have accepted the help of his disciples. But Jesus has a higher purpose, the fulfillment of his Father's will. As we have seen already, Jesus has won his inner battle; it is now only a matter of going through it. Jesus is not to be deterred, his purpose is not to be deflected, even by his well-meaning friends.

When do you have such firm purpose? When have you had such a firm conviction about carrying out God's will for you? If you have a weaker sense of purpose, are you not avoiding God's will—saying, in effect, "Oh, good. My friends want to help me out of this unpleasantness. I guess I should let them."

Carrying a cross as Jesus did is not for weaklings. It is not for those who look for excuses to take an easier way. It is for the strong and the committed, those who put the love of God and deep devotion to obedience above all other considerations in life.

Jesus and the Sanhedrin

The historical problems with Jesus' interrogation by members of the Sanhedrin (the Jewish ruling council) are considerable. First, read the stories in Matthew 26:57-68, Mark 14:53-

65, Luke 22:66-71. By Jewish Law, the Sanhedrin was not supposed to meet at night, as Matthew and Mark indicate, so it is unlikely that the whole council convened to examine Jesus, in spite of Mark's suggestion. (In Luke, however, they wait for daylight to convene the whole council.) Furthermore, in Matthew and Mark, it is clear that the interrogation took place in the house of the high priest—also legally questionable. In Matthew and Mark, the story actually reads more like a cloak-and-dagger event than a public trial. These discrepancies cannot be resolved, but they affect the inner content of the event very little.

Once you have the stories well in mind, please consider the following ideas.

In Matthew and Mark, Jesus at first does not reply to his questioners. Some of the testimony against him is indicated, but Jesus says nothing. The stories are almost certainly shortened versions of any actual events, just to suggest (as the gospel writers maintain) that the evidence was concocted or irrelevant and that Jesus was innocent.

In Matthew and Mark, the leaders and false witnesses try to demonstrate that Jesus spoke *against* the Temple, which was a punishable crime, but even that doesn't succeed.

In Luke, the story is shorter and not quite so harsh. Jesus is not silent, but neither does he answer directly their question about messiahship. Luke goes directly to the point for which Jesus was finally condemned in all three Synoptics: blasphemy. He is less interested in the other points made in Matthew or Mark.

When ordered to speak, Jesus does so (Matthew 26:64), and he tells the truth, though couched in language not quite direct—a typical Near Eastern cultural pattern. For his hearers, however, it is a perfectly clear answer; and they immediately know they need call no more witnesses. Jesus has condemned himself out of his own mouth by blaspheming, that is, by equating himself in their minds with the divine Being, the Blessed One. In Judea, blasphemy was punishable by death, specifically by stoning.

The leaders, however, are not inclined to stone him. They only abuse him, then take him to Pilate. Much argument has been advanced over the centuries about whether the Jews could legally have killed Jesus; but regardless of that technicality, they wanted to make the Romans responsible for his death. We are not told specifically why. We know already that the priests were afraid of how the people would react to their proceedings against Jesus. Perhaps they assumed that if Pilate ordered him killed, the people would not blame their own leaders.

For Your Reflection

In the trial scene, we notice two remarkable aspects of Jesus' character—aspects we as disciples are invited to imitate. One is his disinterest in personal self-defense; the other is his commitment to truth, even at his own peril.

Jesus is silent about all the false witnesses. When are we silent under accusation? Some people, it is true, do use silence as a weapon of counterattack. They are recognized in psychology as "passive-aggressive" and are hard to relate to because their silence is fundamentally dishonest. That, however, is not what Jesus is doing here.

Most people jump to their own personal defense quite quickly and vociferously, *especially* when the accusation is false. Court scenes are not usual for us, but family challenges are familiar to all. Take a look at your family relationships to find out how you usually respond to blame. Is your reaction different when the accusation is true than when it is false?

Jesus' silence may have a still deeper motive for us to

ponder. He simply had no need to defend himself from accusations, true or false, because in his heart he knew who he was, what he was doing, and that he was obedient to God.

How could one of us be so certain, so centered, so open? Once again, we must learn to move beyond egocentric interests. Then there is no need to prove the slightest thing about ourselves to anyone else. If our desires, our love, the center of our lives, is God and not ourselves, defense of our little selves when we are accused is almost irrelevant.

Here is a caution, however. To refuse to prove ourselves right because we are *afraid* to act, or because we think we *should* not, will cause us emotional difficulty. Such challenging behavior as nondefensiveness in personal relationships should never be superimposed on a weakened sense of selfhood. Rather, it flows from inner strength.

Jesus' nondefensive behavior points to a profound inner condition. We try to develop this depth for our own spiritual growth: to actually *be* so profoundly centered on God that self-defense is not even interesting. To *be* so steady in heart is quite different from forcing ourselves to behave as if we were when we're not!

So be sure not to take this point (or any of the others) from the passion as an example of behavior to be blindly copied. Rather, each point indicates inner possibilities for us as we grow more and more into the life of God. Then the behavior is spontaneous, unforced, genuine—as Jesus' behavior was.

Second, when he did speak, Jesus spoke the truth. Only truth mattered to him. He did not consider consequences important, although he surely knew that what he said to the Sanhedrin leaders was going to make matters worse. Can you imagine that Jesus would lie *for any reason* at all?

We are inclined to think that we also do not lie, that we speak only the truth. Or that if we do lie, we are somehow justified in it. Yet the deepest spiritual tradition in Christianity says, "If you speak, say only the truth. If you can't or don't wish to tell the truth, keep silent."

Most of us may not, in fact, tell blatant lies. But are we authentically truthful? Is truthfulness our aim in all our speech? Check yourself for these possibilities.

- Do you speak in such a way as to let others think you know something you really don't know? When you don't know, do you say simply, "I don't know"?

- Do you ever repeat stories about people which you have not verified firsthand?

- If you feel threatened, do you try to protect yourself by saying things that are not quite true (including shifting possible blame in another direction)? If this is one of your personal weaknesses, ponder long on Jesus' interrogation with an open heart.

- Do you exaggerate your stories to dramatize your life or to impress others? Someone once said a story worth telling is a story worth exaggerating, which tickles our funny bone. But is an exaggerated story the truth?

- In close relationships and in relating to children, are you totally truthful and open? Why or why not, do you think?

If you approach the practice of truthfulness as a moral issue only, you will have difficulty. We all know that we're not "supposed to" lie, and most of us make exceptions for tact or "white lies." Total truthfulness is a particular spiritual practice, never taken up because one "should." If you do that, you can develop unhealthy compulsions and scruples that won't lead you to any peace.

If, however, you think of truthfulness as a means to something wonderful—becoming close to the Lord and being a fully worthy disciple—then whatever you choose about the truth will not condemn you. If you choose to be truthful, you will move faster toward your goal. If you choose to lie in some degree, you slow yourself down. When you think in this way, guilt will not paralyze you and your heart will be open to the cleansing of honest remorse (as you will soon see with Peter).

As you practice deeper and deeper truthfulness, you will discover a simplicity about your speech—and about your life—that may be new. When we speak directly and truly, we don't have to constantly calculate the effects of our speech or whether we should say this or that. It gets very easy: if we wish to tell the truth, we speak; if we do not wish to tell the truth, we keep silent.

Of course, other people may or may not believe us, even so. But their response is not under our control anyway and is really not our business. Our business is to seek truthfulness for the sake of our love of the Lord, just as Jesus was truthful because of his love of God.

In the end, you will find that truthfulness is easier than any other way—and it makes for a lovely, clean feeling in the heart.

Peter Again

In Matthew 26:69-75 and Mark 14:66-72, Peter's denials follow the scene at the Sanhedrin. In Luke 22:54-65, the order is reversed, but the essence of the two scenes remains much the same. Reread now the stories of Peter's denials of the Lord.

Don't we all love Peter? He is so passionate about Jesus. He *wants* to be good. He wants to understand. He has a generous heart. He wants to be close to Jesus forever. Yet when his own test comes, he fails.

Some people find Peter comforting, thinking that if Peter failed and could still be loved by Jesus, then their own failures will not separate them from the Lord, either. That is true. They won't.

My personal response to the failure of Peter—and of all the disciples during the passion (in the Synoptics)—is a little different. I look at Peter's failure under pressure, and it reminds me all too quickly of the ease with which I am knocked off my own path to God. Yes, with the grace of the Lord, I crawl back on again, but I can fall off so fast! It's scary to see how fragile I am.

Peter is completely unaware that he is "off" until it's all over and the words of his denials hang forever in the air, unretrievable, to sear his soul probably for the rest of his life, even after Jesus forgave him.

What was the nature of the pressure that caused Peter to collapse? If you are uncertain, take another look at the stories, then continue reading here.

Peter may have thought that his life or his freedom was threatened. Or perhaps he was simply afraid of other people's negative opinions. Plenty of people are very much afraid of that. Whatever his precise fears, however, we can see that Peter was only concerned about himself. Disciple though he was, and even though he loved Jesus and wanted to be with him always, his first concern was still—himself. So he had nothing large enough, strong enough, to sustain him when that little self seemed threatened.

How much are we like Peter?

Isn't Peter's self-centeredness, that is, his basic orientation toward himself, what Jesus asks his disciples to give up? "Deny yourself" probably does not mean merely giving up coffee or candy. It means displacing oneself from the center of one's interest and placing the Lord there. This is a huge aim! It can never be completed overnight because it has many layers of subtlety that we cannot see until we arrive at them.

At the least, it means being willing to ask in every circumstance, "What is true? What is kind? What is the Lord's teaching in this situation?" And then trying to follow up with action on whatever one does understand.

And it means one more thing. Peter got caught in his denials at a moment when Jesus was out of sight. I don't know if the gospel writers intended this, but it strikes me that if we let God "out of our sight," that is, if we forget his presence to us, we are forced to decide and to act on our own. Then we are most likely to fail.

God does not put challenges or lessons before us and then abandon us to our own inadequacies. God stays right there with us, within us, to give us strength. But we must remember God. We must ask for his help. We must open ourselves to receive God's grace to carry the immediate form of our cross. If we don't reach out to him, how can he give us what we need?

Second, notice Peter's reaction when he realizes what he has done—and what he has not been able to do. Sudden tears of intense and honest remorse are among the Lord's great gifts to those who desire to know him. When we see, without pretense and without veil, exactly how we have violated the goodness or love that we ourselves most desire, lasting cleansing can occur. Perhaps that is why Jesus let Peter go through the pain.

Remorse is not like guilt, which is paralyzing. Remorse is clean; it burns like fire and takes away the egocenteredness of feeling guilty. Remorse cannot be produced by decision. It springs up in a sincere heart that knows undeniably its own weakness.

Those of us who truly want to follow Jesus will put the aim

of discipleship firmly before our mind and heart and will actively pursue it. Steady effort will eventually be rewarded with closeness to the Lord, but along the way error and—by the grace of God—remorse will enter our experience. Our part is not to flee the cleansing fire but to remain present to it and burn or weep honestly in the face of our own failures.

For Your Reflection

- How do we respond to others' poor opinions of us or blame of us or other suggestions that we may not be as good as we want to be? Do we capitulate to other people to make sure to keep their good opinion of us? When have we felt remorse deep enough for tears?

- God's help is ready instantly to strengthen us in any challenge, in all threat or misfortune or pain. Do we ask him to help us?

Jesus, Pilate, and the Crowd

Again, begin by reading the scenes: Matthew 27:1-31 (verses 3-10 are about the death of Judas but do not relate directly to Jesus' passion. This passage is unique to Matthew.), Mark 15:1-20, Luke 23:1-25.

When the scene shifts from the Sanhedrin to Pilate, we are in another world. The Sanhedrin was a kind of advisory council and supreme court for the Jews in those areas where the Romans allowed them to make their own decisions. The highest position in Judea that could be held by a Jew was high priest. All Judean leaders were ultimately responsible to the Roman governor, who at this time was Pontius Pilate.

In the Sanhedrin, Jesus had been among his own people. They shared with him a common religious and cultural tradition. Pilate represented the Romans, who had almost nothing in common with the Jews. The accusations against Jesus at the Sanhedrin were religious; before Pilate, they were intentionally political—Pilate had no interest in religious questions.

Jesus before Pilate, in the Synoptics, says almost nothing (in high contrast to the scene in John, which we'll examine in the next chapter). He offers only a few affirmative words to Pilate, then keeps silence for the rest of the scene. He does not answer accusations against him.

In Matthew, this portrayal may reflect the Suffering Servant of Isaiah—passages which the earliest Christians understood in the light of Jesus' passion. Two verses that you may find especially interesting are Isaiah 52:15 and 53:7.

In Luke, the accent seems to lie on the injustice of the proceedings. Anyone who had read Luke up to this point would know that the charges made against Jesus in Luke 23:2-5 are simply not true. He did not say that one should not pay taxes; he did not say that he was a political king. Though he surely aroused people, it was for goodness and for love, not for sedition. Though Pilate does not know Jesus' story, he sees that these charges are false.

In the scene of Jesus' questioning by Pilate, in contrast to his appearance before the Sanhedrin, there is a crowd of people. We do not know who they are or even exactly where this "trial" was held. Crowds gathered easily in Jerusalem during festival seasons. The importance of the crowd here, however, is that all three gospels affirm that the *people* of Israel (the Jews) did not understand or accept Jesus.

This view expresses only some of the facts. It was influenced by events in the decades after Jesus' death. In actuality, all of Jesus' first followers were Jews. Enough Jews followed him to threaten the Jewish leadership. That had to be more than a handful. As we have already seen, however, by the time Luke and Matthew were written, tensions between the young Christian communities and the Jewish faith were high, as were tensions between Jewish Christians and gentile Christians. Christianity was trying to find its identity in relation to its tradition as well as to current circumstances.

Theologically, the crowd's response recalls the Old Testament pattern of prophet after prophet being rejected or ignored. Now the latest and greatest of them is also rejected. This is a decisive turning point in the history of the relationship between Yahweh and Israel, according to the gospel writers. With this last rejection, the glorious gifts of Yahweh are offered for the first time to the Gentiles, who became, then, the New Israel.

The rejection of Jesus is heightened by the people's choice of Jesus Barabbas to be set free. Note the irony of his name. He and Jesus probably shared a first name, and *Barabbas* means "son of Abba," or son of the father. Barabbas was a revolutionary, jailed for murder in the course of insurrection. So the choice was not only a choice between condemned men but between ways of life—then and now. Does one follow Jesus' way of love and inner power or the way of nationalism, violence, and external power? The crowd's choice was clear. In Barabbas, they may have seen a national hero in chains.

For Your Reflection

The question that necessarily arises out of the scene with Pilate is a complex and difficult one. When we suffer injustice, violence, or the threat of violence, how are we called to respond? Try not to assume that you already know, and treat yourself to a long and thoughtful consideration of this issue. (This is more than the matter of accusation in personal relationships that we have already considered.)

Consider the following points in your reflection.

- Jesus says nothing and does not defend himself at all. Is he intended to be an example for us?

- What was Jesus' purpose in allowing violence against himself?

- What is our purpose in affirming our "right to self-defense" against violence or injustice?

- What kind of person does it take to suffer violence or injustice in love and in silence? Are you interested in becoming that kind of person?

- Might there be ways of defending oneself or struggling for high values in society that do not involve attacking other people but that involve the power of intense love—as intense as Jesus' love—in our own hearts? If so, how can we develop that level of love?

- Is there an important difference between personal victimization and social victimization? Is a Christian woman who is battered called to the same response as a Christian parish with crime inside its borders?

You may think of many other questions and points on the subject of violence, injustice, and self-defense. No one can answer *for* you. I urge you, however, not to answer automatically but to reexamine the questions in the light of Jesus' passion.

The choices implied in the trial before Pilate reach in other directions as well. Place yourself in the crowd for a few minutes. Now think about the following questions.

- If and when national interests conflict with the way of Jesus, which have you chosen? Which would you choose now? Why?

- When an issue has a popular response that is less than Jesus' quality of life, which do you choose? Why?
- Do you choose or advocate violence over nonviolence in these areas of your life: entertainment (movies and TV programs) and the judicial system (capital punishment and crime prevention)?
- In personal emotional crises, are your words vitriolic or do you calm down before you respond?

Now look again at what Pilate does, familiar though it is. He thinks Jesus is innocent. He says so. But the people disregard him. He capitulates to them—probably to keep the peace or simply to get them out of his hair. Is his a position of integrity?

When you capitulate to someone (even your spouse) and betray your own perception, giving in merely to close the issue, what happens to your integrity? What about Jesus' example throughout the passion? Does he keep his integrity? Are we or are we not invited to be like him? Do we want to be like him?

The Mockery of the Soldiers

The soldiers are not interested in Jesus or in the issues at hand. They are merely taunting somebody handy to entertain themselves in what must have been a stressful and largely boring job. Judean military service was not a plum assignment!

However, the *way* they mock Jesus is significant in the gospels. They ridicule him with the accouterments of kingship: the purple robe, the crown, the reed scepter. They kneel to him and mock him as king.

As happens so often in the gospels, the mockery of the soldiers is ironic. They are telling the truth—Jesus is a king, although not the kind they know. His kingship is in another "place" than the throne room, and his policies are not those of ordinary political power. So their mockery, unknown to themselves, points to the reality of Jesus' royalty.

For Your Reflection

Mocking people is largely out of fashion today. Those who used to come in for social and personal ridicule are now considered minorities with a legitimate and insistent claim to respect. That is exactly as it should be.

Yet mockery is not gone from human consciousness by any means. Is it utterly gone from your own? Do you make fun of people for any reason at all? Do you ridicule people in the privacy of your thoughts or words—or your own living room? Do you speak or think scornfully of anyone?

Often, mockery is born in our recognition of another's weakness along with our unconscious feelings of weakness in ourselves. We do it to make ourselves seem stronger in our own eyes. It doesn't work, of course. Ridiculing another's weakness only increases our own and makes our blindness deeper. The old cliché "It takes one to know one" is totally true.

On the other hand, how do we handle it when someone maliciously ridicules us? (Affectionate teasing is not the question here; it's motivated quite differently.) If it comes from people we love, is it a different experience than when it comes from a slight acquaintance or a stranger? What difference does it make to us if mockery happens in public or in private?

This scene is a good one to enter imaginatively for your own prayer. Become a mocking soldier. Get into it! Let yourself feel what they seem to have felt. Notice if the feeling is familiar. Notice if you want to keep the feeling. Turn your recognitions into prayer.

Then be in Jesus' place, in physical pain and being mocked. What do you feel? What do you think about? How do you react? Then turn these perceptions of yourself into prayer also.

The Way of the Cross

Of the three Synoptics, Luke's "way" includes the most detail. Read Matthew 27:32, Mark 15:21, and Luke 23:26-31. You will immediately notice that only some of the incidents in the traditional Stations of the Cross are based in Scripture (John's gospel adds no detail). The Stations are the fruit of pious reflection in later centuries than Jesus' own.

The Synoptics note that Jesus had help with his cross; a man who just happened to be there was pushed into it by the Roman soldiers. Only Mark mentions that Simon was the father of two men, apparently known to his community.

Luke adds to the scene a large crowd of predominantly compassionate bystanders, mostly Jews in Jerusalem for the festival, who follow along with Jesus. In the crowd are women who mourn over him in the traditional Jewish manner. Jesus pauses to warn them that their grief should be for themselves because terrible times are ahead for Jerusalem. His words to them are not consolation but a warning, a foretelling of judgment, much like the Old Testament prophetic judgment on a recalcitrant people.

By the time Luke wrote, the Jewish war of A.D. 66-70 was over. Jerusalem and the Temple were devastated. Luke's community, therefore, would have instantly recognized that Jesus' prediction was fulfilled. They probably interpreted it as God's judgment on the city that could have glorified the Messiah but rejected him instead. Yet the women to whom Jesus speaks are "on his side." Are they to experience the coming judgment?

For Your Reflection

The Bible testifies repeatedly to the universal truth that there are consequences in human life for error—even when that error is not malicious. These words of Jesus belong to that testimony. The individual women are not "guilty," yet Jesus warns them to weep for themselves; terrors are coming.

Societal emphasis on the value of the individual and individual experience is largely a modern Western notion. People in biblical times would have understood that the group or the community has a definite identity from which their own identity took its reality. If the group acts erroneously, then the group suffers consequences that may affect individuals who did not actually participate in the error. The Bible accepts the idea that we are members of each other and that each is affected by each of the others—for joy or for pain.

Reflect, then, on the following questions.

- How much responsibility do you accept for group decisions? in the family? in the parish? in the city or nation?
- Do you expect to benefit from the good decisions and to escape the painful results of poor decisions?
- Might it be time for us to recover some sense of group identity or group responsibility so our society is less an aggregate of individuals and more cohesively a community? What do you think?

The Crucifixion

The details of the crucifixion are remarkably stark, especially in Mark. Again, more details are given in Luke, and the differences make definite points. Read about the crucifixion in Matthew 27:33-44, Mark 15:22-32, and Luke 23:33-43.

Notice that in Mark and Matthew, Jesus is mocked again by the Jewish leaders as well as by the revolutionaries crucified alongside Jesus. The mockery centers around the inscription of Jesus' "crime"—he is "king of the Jews." The revilers also dare him to save himself from death on the cross, since he demonstrated power in his public ministry.

There is no relief from the horror in Mark or in Matthew. Even though Jesus is offered a mild painkiller, he refuses it—and, of course, he does not reply to the mockery. In supreme irony, the soldiers gamble for Jesus' clothes—the last stripping away of any human dignity. In these two gospels, the crucifixion emphasizes again the suffering, rejected Messiah by putting his true titles into the mouths of his opponents: Messiah and King of Israel in Mark, King of Israel and Son of God in Matthew.

As usual, Luke handles the whole scene somewhat more gently. Except for the offer of a drug, Luke includes the same details as Mark and Matthew. Other details are added, however, that change the quality of Jesus' participation in the crucifixion.

The dialogue with the two revolutionaries on their crosses is unique to Luke. He tells the story to reveal again that Jesus responds to the honest, repentant person who recognizes his or her own wrongs and asks for compassion. Notice that the criminal Jesus forgives will have no chance to "make up" for his wrongs. He is only compassionate to Jesus and just in his estimate of himself. He commends himself to the mercy of the Lord.

Luke thus affirms that in his very dying, Jesus still offers immediate transformation and salvation to those who long for it. In the midst of mocking rejection and in great pain, Jesus' compassion dominates everything else.

For Your Reflection

Only in Luke does Jesus pray for forgiveness for his tormentors. This occurs right after the nails are driven. Compassion and forgiveness for his torturers is so stupendous an act that it demands pondering.

Look again at the scene and consider the following questions.

- On what does such forgiveness depend? Does it depend on whether the receiver deserves it? Does it depend on whether the wrongdoer can be justified in some way? Does it depend on the character of the forgiver? Is a person's character independent of circumstances? Can one act according to one's nature or habits regardless of what is happening?

- Looking at the compassion of Jesus just from the human standpoint, how do you think he was able to do it?

- Now ponder your own living in the light of your present understanding of Jesus. How big a part of your character is compassion? Where does it come from? Would you like to be more compassionate? How might you increase the intensity of your compassion?

Think about the above questions before reading further.

Some people—myself included—find that compassion cannot be fostered directly. I may understand how another person got to be the way she or he is, I may feel a certain sympathy for or be willing to justify the person's wrongs in terms of her or his own past experience. But this does not produce compassion. Compassion has another source: God, who *is* pure compassion.

So consider this: the closer one lives to the heart of God, the more compassion flows naturally through one's own heart. For the person who lives as close to God as Jesus did, compassion is the only possible stance; it has become that person's own nature. Such a person expresses compassion, then, regardless of what is happening to the personal self—his or her own situation doesn't enter the matter at all. Compassion simply *is*.

We may have a long way to grow into compassion so God can make our very being as compassionate as Jesus' was. But isn't it worth some prayer, some practice, some reflection? And couldn't we begin by forgiving those whose hurtful actions are much less malicious than what Jesus experienced—those everyday hurts when someone says something ugly or doesn't live up to our expectations or causes a painful injustice? Each such act of forgiveness will draw us closer to God, and one day the Lord's own compassion may flow as naturally through us as through the Son. If you desire that, begin to practice forgiveness right now.

The Death of Jesus

The account of Jesus' death is found in Matthew 27:45-56, Mark 15:33-41, and Luke 23:44-49. The darkness over the whole land suggests that *this* dying has universal implications, the momentary victory of the forces of darkness.

In Matthew and Mark, Jesus cries out the first line of Psalm 22, "My God, my God, why have you forsaken me?" A superficial glance might suggest that Jesus felt utterly abandoned by God. Of course, we cannot guess his inner experience. However, most scholars think that Jesus was recalling here the whole of Psalm 22. Pause and read Psalm 22 now.

This psalm is a lament over the psalmist's own miseries but also a profound expression of faith in Yahweh. With the honesty typical of the Old Testament, complaints to God and trust in God appear almost in the same breath. The Old

Testament writers face their troubles directly and admit their suffering but trust in God anyway. The whole of the psalm gives this picture, so it is most appropriate to Jesus on the cross.

Notice that Luke includes not Psalm 22 but Psalm 31:6. Psalm 31 is also a lament but a gentler one. In line with his consistent view, Luke sees Jesus in a primarily trustful and self-giving relationship with the Father. So his dying is simpler. In the midst of the eclipse, he cries out in trust and ceases to breathe. There is less mocking, no misunderstanding of the *"Eli, Eli"* as in Matthew and Mark.

All three Synoptics include the detail of the curtain or veil of the sanctuary being ripped from top to bottom. This veil hung between the court of sacrifice and the Holy of Holies, which was entered only once a year by one priest and where the divine Presence was "localized" for the Jewish people. Its tearing is one of the signs that accompany Jesus' death.

Scholars do not agree on the exact meaning of this symbol. It might be a judgment against the Temple, whose leaders have rejected Jesus in the very moment of his dying. Matthew and Luke were both written after the Temple was destroyed, so they might have found judgment appropriate. Mark includes it also. In his time, the Temple still stood, though this fact would not preclude a Marcan judgment against it.

A second possibility may be that the tearing of the Temple curtain symbolized the presence of God, now made accessible to all people through the death of Jesus. We cannot know the intention of the tradition, but symbols being what they are, neither meaning is to be excluded.

One of the most important points around Jesus' death is that it evoked a confession of faith from the Roman centurion— "captain of the crucifixion detail," as Father Donald Senior has put it. In Mark, the soldier responds to the manner of Jesus' death—that in the weakness of his dying cry, something was touched in the soldier's heart. In Matthew, the soldier responds to all the signs—the darkness, the earthquake, and so on. In Luke, the reason is not so clear but may have been the trust expressed by Jesus with his last cry.

The idea common to all three gospels is that precisely in his dying, Jesus evokes faith in the hearts of onlookers, specifically in a gentile heart. The earliest Christians especially cherished Jesus' death because of this understanding. Their life with God began (or began anew) with Jesus' death. Yes, the resurrection mattered, but his death opened the way to God for them.

Notice also the presence of the women in all three gospels—followers of Jesus from Galilee who watched faithfully from a distance. Some of them would return to try to serve Jesus in his tomb—and find the resurrection instead. No mention is made of his male followers being present, although Luke speaks of "friends" with the women and the crowds who mourn him as they leave.

For Your Reflection

Since the Synoptic Gospel accounts do not agree totally (and John's is even more different), we cannot recover the exact historical details of Jesus' death. That fact is hard for many of us to accept. A person's last words, last experiences, and manner of dying usually matter to us. Even if the details are painful, we cherish them.

So once again, we are invited to concentrate on the meaning of Jesus' death for ourselves. The Christian tradition from earliest times found the death of Jesus to be redemptive. It has been the source of intense reflection and prayer as well as a favorite subject of painters and sculptors throughout the centuries. Pilgrims still travel to the place tradition says the crucifixion occurred, just as people visit the graves of their loved ones.

Take time to place yourself imaginatively in one of these situations. You might sit on the ground before the cross and hear the voices of Jesus and the crowd and watch their movements. You might watch with the women from a distance. Or you might visit the empty hill as you imagine it would be after Jesus died.

Ponder, easily and slowly, what the death of Jesus has actually meant in your own life. Do not try to force yourself to feel sad or to feel any other particular feeling. Instead, focus on the meaning of his death for you. Your thoughts are a personal reflection; they need not have heavy theological implications. How have you thought about Jesus' death? felt about it? How might your life be different if Jesus had not been killed?

Now consider whether this reflection has changed anything in your thoughts or feelings. Allow yourself to be with what you have learned. Quietly get to know yourself a little more in relation to Jesus' death. Perhaps you will wish to "take it in" a bit more thoroughly than you have until now.

When you have taken this reflection to completion, turn it into prayer, if you haven't already. Speak to Jesus himself about his death, and express your feelings and thoughts to him.

The Burial of Jesus

After the noise, the shouting, and the drama of the passion and crucifixion, after the hurrying here and there, the wrenching pain, and the final breath, comes a quiet. In that quiet, Jesus is buried. Read about it in Matthew 27:57-66, Mark 15:42-47, and Luke 23:50-56.

Each gospel includes a unique detail about Jesus' burial. Mark speaks about Pilate's amazement that Jesus died so quickly; the agony of crucifixion was not usually over in a mere few hours but could last for days. Matthew says Pilate put a guard at the tomb. This information may have assured Matthew's community that Jesus had truly died—a fact that had been challenged before Matthew's time. Luke gives a little more detail about the women than either Mark or Matthew.

The participation of Joseph of Arimathea is noteworthy. He was willing to associate himself publicly with a condemned criminal—a courageous act indeed, since such association could also lead to legal action. Yet he is described as a disciple only in Matthew. Mark and Luke say that he was a righteous member of the Sanhedrin—a second reason for caution on his part, which he ignored in order to honor Jesus' body.

The women are present at the burial, taking note of the tomb's location or watching (especially in Matthew) in fidelity to their love for Jesus.

For Your Reflection

In prayerful attention, place yourself at the tomb of Jesus as you would beside the new grave of a loved one in your personal life. Just be there. Respond exactly as you wish—with silence, with prayer, with love, or with whatever is your own honest experience.

So far as you know, as you watch the sealing of the tomb, this is the end of something beautiful. How does it affect you? A particular question you might ask yourself is whether you would have the courage of a Joseph.

Be willing to accept the pain in the burial, if you experience any. If you don't, just be peaceful here by the garden tomb. Try not to jump ahead to the dramatic comfort of the resurrection. Jesus' passion is over. He is dead and buried. In the quiet around the tomb, seek your own heart.

CHAPTER THREE

The Passion in John

Moving from the Synoptic Gospels to the Gospel of John is almost like entering a new world. Much is familiar, and yet the atmosphere is much more exalted, more mystical. You may review the comments on John in Chapter One, page 16.

The Gospel of John sees in Jesus the eternal Word of God (John 1:1-5,10-14,16-18). Its sublime view influences every aspect of its portrayal of Jesus, and the passion is no exception. By story, explanation, irony, and drama, John explores the full meaning of Jesus.

Since John's gospel is unique unto itself, comparison with the Synoptics is quite complex. So rather than including a section-by-section comparison, we will discuss the passion in John in this chapter and relationships that may be drawn between John and the Synoptics in Chapter Four. For the writers, there seems to have been no relationship.

The purpose of John's gospel is to inspire faith in Jesus. John's understanding of faith is extraordinarily rich. Even so, faith in Jesus is only the beginning of the profound and exciting spiritual adventure envisioned by John. Open to all believers, this adventure is a journey toward becoming "children of God" (John 1:12) and ultimately implies full oneness with the Father of Jesus. Along the way, faith in Jesus expands and deepens, as understanding also grows. Relationship with Jesus also expands to include not only serving the Lord but also loving friendship and, finally, union with him.

Anticipating the Passion

Throughout the gospel, John points forward to the glorification of Jesus in and through his passion and death. Although John hints that Jesus is a sacrificial lamb, his overwhelming portrait of Jesus presents a master, one who is totally in charge and who in full power has given his life in love to the Father for the sake of his followers. From this angle, the passion is not a victimization at all. The passion in John is an enthronement and a victory, a fulfillment and a treasure, for Jesus himself.

In your reflection on the passion in John, you will benefit greatly if you read it straight through as if it were the only information you have about the passion (John 13–19). Try not to fill in the gaps, though you may wonder why a few beloved and familiar events are not included. By reading freshly, you will feel John's understanding of the passion tradition. Comparison can come later.

Now let's look together at the passion in John.

The Last Supper

At Jesus' last meal with his disciples, we find conversation, the prediction of Judas' betrayal, the prediction of Peter's denials, and Jesus washing the feet of the disciples. Then follow four chapters of discourses, or long speech and prayer, by Jesus himself. Read or reread Chapters 13–17 now so they will be keen in your mind.

Notice the introduction (verses 1-2). The public ministry is over. Jesus has come to his long-expected "hour" when he will glorify the Father by his final obedience and return to him. Jesus loves his own right to the end. Judas is set to betray him. Everything is ready.

Then we read three of the most moving verses in the whole Gospel of John: 13:3-5. Dwell on them. In this astounding fullness, in this position of universal power, what did Jesus do? He washed the feet of his disciples.

The Master, who could have commanded them to do anything he wished, whose power extended even to life and death (he had raised Lazarus in Chapter 11), who is facing his own immediate death—this Master of all performs a simple, loving, humble courtesy for his disciples. He *serves* them in a way familiar to them, yet made radically new by the Master's hands.

Washing of feet was a slave's work. In Jesus' time and place, the feet were the most disgraceful part of the body. No one normally even touched another person's shoes. Only the "lowest" person could be expected to cleanse another's feet from the dirt of the road.

We do not have this intense feeling about feet in general today. If you have ever participated in a feet-washing, however, you know that it is not necessarily easy to accept, even today. The gesture bears an intrinsic humility: kneeling before another to care for his or her feet. It is also humbling for the sensitive recipient because we are otherwise so intent on our own self-sufficiency.

Peter, in his usual honest way, objects for exactly that reason. His beloved *Master* wants to serve him most humbly. He cannot accept it at first. Yet when he understands that it expresses the closeness between Master and disciple, Peter wants a whole bath!

The Master, who is everything, serves the disciples. All through the gospel, Jesus serves people, though we hardly notice it. At the wedding at Cana, Jesus provides wine for an embarrassed host. When Nicodemus arrives in the middle of the night with a burning question, Jesus holds a long conversation with him. Jesus cures a man long paralyzed at the pool of Bethesda. He feeds hungry people. He gives sight to the man born blind. He speaks of himself as a shepherd who takes care of the sheep. And, of course, he gives Lazarus back his life. The major events in John 1–11 are Jesus' acts of service, enhanced by teaching.

Since the Gospel of John emphasizes the spiritual possibilities in discipleship, all these acts of Jesus may symbolize his service to our spiritual growth. The purpose of his very life—and his death—was to bring those who desire God into close relationship and even union with God. Jesus serves our spiritual development because he *wants* us to be one with him, with one another, and with the Father. (See John 17:20-21.) The question is, Do we accept his service, do we want for ourselves the oneness with God that he wants for us?

After Jesus had washed their feet, he urged the disciples to take care of one another in the same way. (See John 13:12-17.) Jesus did not literally command for all time that we physically wash one another's feet—even though the commandment is reenacted literally every Holy Thursday. Rather, Jesus meant that we could be as willing as he was to care for one another with great love, in little ways and humble ways as well as in our larger needs. If, like Peter, we finally accept his service to ourselves, how can we not actively look for ways to pass such service along to other people?

For Your Reflection

• How often do we think of Jesus as servant to us? And in what way? We are exhorted to worship him as Lord, to honor him as Master, to believe in him as Son of God. But when do we allow him freely to serve us?

Ponder carefully all your experiences of Jesus serving you: all the gifts he gives, all the help you receive, all the beauties of your life, all the hopes fulfilled. Make a list as long as you can of service you have accepted from the Lord. What is your natural response? Make a prayer of it.

Now consider simple, humble service. We so often give money to the Church, but do we sweep its carpets? We respond when someone dies, but do we visit them when they are alive? We hug someone when we meet them on the street, but do we turn off the TV when they come to our home? We say we are all brothers and sisters, but do we make kindly small talk in an elevator? We belong to the same parish, but...you get the idea.

We fail to see possibilities for service simply because we are not looking for *humble little* kindnesses we can do. We do not value them enough—even as much as clean feet. Take a few minutes to examine your routine. Find half a dozen opportunities to serve another by a small new act. Forget about yourself, your embarrassment, your "I-don't-know-what-to-say" habit. Forget about whether they *deserve* it (after all, Jesus washed Judas' feet). Just uncover opportunities to imitate the service of Jesus. Then do them—and thus fulfill his command of love.

The Supper Continues

Jesus continues to direct the beginnings of his passion. (See

John 13:21-30.) It seems that not all the disciples understood what was happening. Jesus urges Judas to be about his business.

Notice that Jesus, in 13:30, stays open to Judas right to the end, giving him food from the table. Judas accepts it—how could he refuse it from Jesus' own hand? Then "it was night," John says.

In this gospel, night symbolizes the forces of darkness that have opposed Jesus from very early in his ministry. This brief sentence tells us that the darkness is now unrelieved. The reader knows that something ominous is about to happen. Tension rises. In the midst of this darkness, Jesus gives the disciples a new commandment: to love one another as he loved them.

Then Peter's denial (also part of the night) is predicted, against his vociferous protest.

For Your Reflection

Is it an accident that Jesus' commandment of love is placed between the two incidents of darkness? It's hard to find any accidents in John's gospel. Is love commanded in this placement perhaps because the writer knew that "darkness" had continued in the world, in spite of Jesus' victory? and that all people faithful to Jesus would have to try to keep his command in the midst of that darkness?

Love for one another is the mark of the disciples. How much effort do we expend trying to fulfill this particular, unique command of Jesus?

One application of this commandment is the mutual love of disciples within the parish. You may wish to think about the quality of your participation in your parish. How well do you love your fellow parishioners? How do you express your love for them? How might you deepen your love for them? Do you offer your support and sharing to those who are not your "natural" friends or whom you do not know?

If we love Jesus, even a little, we can surely assume that all the parishioners love Jesus, at least a little (of course there always have been differences in intensity of discipleship). If we all love Jesus and accept his love for us, how can we not express that same love to one another?

The Last Discourses

A whole volume of meditations could be written on John 14–17. These four chapters present the essence of John's understanding of Jesus and his disciples and of the possibilities to which all disciples are invited. The chapters are written almost in circles. The main ideas come around again and again in different formulations, with different emphases.

The Last Discourses are wonderful for the prayer of *lectio divina*. They are perfect for reflective, attentive reading. They open inward to ever-deeper understandings.

For Your Reflection

You are invited to discover the Last Discourses for yourself. To help you structure your discoveries, here is a list of ideas to look for.

1. Untroubled hearts and peacefulness
2. The relationship of master and disciple
3. Oneness of Jesus and the Father, Jesus and the disciple, the Father and the disciple
4. Jesus' joy and the disciple
5. The Spirit (or Advocate or Paraclete)
6. How to remain close to Jesus

7. What the disciples may expect after Jesus returns to the
Father

Take a sheet of paper for each of the ideas and copy out
related references as you find them. Or you might color-code
the ideas and underline them in your Bible (this may get
complicated, though, as overlapping occurs).
Then ponder the following questions.

- Which of these sets of verses mean the most to me right
now?
- What new insights have I found in the Discourses?
- How do I presently feel about the goal of oneness with Jesus
and the Father?
- What single concrete action can I take to apply an idea from
the Discourses to my daily life?

The Arrest

Following the Discourses, Jesus and his disciples go to the
garden. The arrest takes place in 18:1-14. Almost immediately,
Judas appears with both Temple guards and Roman soldiers.
Jesus wasted not a moment but stepped forward and identified
himself.

His identification means more than a superficial look at the
English translation may tell us. In 18:5 and 8 (and also the
description in verse 6), Jesus says, "I AM." The verb has no
predicate nominative in the Greek. It does not say, for example,
"I am he" or "I am the one." "I AM" is the name of God given
to Moses in Exodus 3:14—the most sacred name of God
throughout the Bible. Jesus' hearers understood his claim immediately, as you can see in verse 6.

Anyone who is "I AM" hardly needs the help of a sword!

Jesus rebukes Peter—not so much for injuring Malchus as for trying to hinder Jesus' obedience to the Father.

Notice that Jesus commands his captors to let his disciples go. Jesus is in full charge here. There is no surprise in Jesus, no protest, and no action on Judas' part. Jesus hands himself over without ado.

For Your Reflection

Recall a time when your sense of purpose was so strong that you knew exactly what to do and did it without worry or hesitation. Maybe a child was in danger, or a spouse. Maybe it was something you wanted so much that circumstances could not affect you. Maybe it was a goal you were determined to reach. As you recall your experience, ponder the power in purpose. When we know what we are about, obstacles melt in our paths.

In his arrest, as always in John, Jesus commands events. He chooses to glorify the Father by his obedience, and nothing can deter him. In fact, he takes strong initiatives to ensure that his aim is not even slowed down. In so doing, he continues to give us a perfect example. Our imitation will not be perfect in the beginning nor for a long time. Yet we can adopt an aim as exalted as his own: total discipleship to culminate in union with Jesus and the Father, just as he wishes.

We can gradually reorganize our living around that aim (if we have never actually done so). When we do want total discipleship to Jesus, when we with full intention set out to let him be our Master, then everything in our life will change, little by little. Sometimes the changes will be made for us, apparently by circumstances but actually set in motion by our own decision—a form of cooperation with the Lord's action in our heart.

Most interesting of all, our perception of life's events

changes in the light of our desire for full discipleship. Everything that happens to us, no matter what quality it seems to have, will be an opportunity to come closer to Jesus and the Father. Nothing will be irrelevant. Everything will have a meaning beyond the obvious. Nothing can "throw" us for long because we keep moving forward, our heart and vision fixed on Jesus, just as he was fixed on the Father.

So now place yourself in the scene of the arrest and remain attentive to what happens there. While watching, ask yourself if you want to follow this Jesus who takes such strong action to obey his Father to the end. Are you interested in becoming a total disciple? More than all else?

Peter's Denial

In 18:15-18, 25-27, we find Peter near a charcoal fire in the courtyard of the high priest. Imagine a scene in a suspense film. Our mental camera zooms in on this charcoal fire. It's a clue, a connection that will become important later on. A charcoal fire appears in only one other place in the New Testament, in one of Jesus' appearances after the resurrection. (See John 21:9.) The two scenes are thus connected. You may wish to read them both to discover why.

Peter's weakness in denying his relationship with Jesus is clear. Something else is equally clear here as well, if we do not take it for granted. Peter is one of only two disciples that have stayed with Jesus after his arrest (the other is unnamed). Where are the rest of them? Peter loved Jesus enough not to flee into the darkness, though not yet enough to risk suffering or denigration for his Master.

For Your Reflection

Aren't we often like Peter? We want to know Jesus, to be in

his vicinity. Still, we are not quite ready to risk much on his behalf—especially not the scornful opinion of others.

- Where inside yourself do you begin to be frightened of "claiming" the Lord? Do you speak freely of him? of your love for him? of your relationship with him? Do your friends at work or on sports teams or at coffee klatsches know that you belong to him? Where is the edge of your own freedom in Jesus?

Peter is available to us in the communion of saints. Perhaps you would like to discuss with him your own reluctance about public association with Jesus.

The Hearing Before Annas

The exchange is brief between Jesus and Annas, the father-in-law of the high priest (and some scholars say the power behind the throne). Read it in 18:19-24.

Notice that although John says Jesus was then taken to Caiaphas, not a word of that meeting is recounted. Because John's story of the passion is similar in outline to the accounts in the Synoptics, it is likely that the main events of the story were firm in the early Christian tradition. It is details and viewpoints that vary. John's passion often omits details that either do not suit its well-defined purpose or that the writer may have assumed his community already knew. Occasionally, John refers symbolically earlier in the gospel to events that the Synoptics put in the passion.

The main characteristic of Jesus before Annas is, again, his natural and definite authority. He does not defend himself in the least but affirms that his teaching has been totally public and need not be probed. One of the guards finds Jesus insolent and hits him in reproach. Jesus asks quietly for proper legal procedure, his poise undisturbed. We are not given the outcome of the inquiry.

Here we see again that Jesus' opponents are unable to recognize in him the truth. Darkness reigns in their hearts—perhaps another reason that this inquiry occurs at night in John.

Jesus Before Pilate

Jesus' encounter with Pilate in John's gospel is one of the most magnificent scenes in the New Testament—for its significance, certainly, but for its sense of theater as well. As you read John 18:28–19:16, imagine the scene as a drama. Try to characterize Jesus in your own imagination.

The scene opens in supreme irony. The leaders are afraid of ritual defilement for entering a gentile building but have no compunctions about handing Jesus over to death (see 18:28). Jesus is inside the praetorium, the Jewish leaders outside. Pilate moves back and forth between the two powers.

The first exchange with the leaders (18:29-31) is a mutual provocation. Jewish leadership and Pilate very much disliked each other but had to get along for political reasons. Their mutual acrimony is evident here. The Jews may be displeased that they cannot execute Jesus themselves. Still, it is crucifixion they want (Jesus has long since announced the manner of his death in John 12:32). For crucifixion, they need Pilate's permission and his soldiers.

Then Pilate goes inside to examine Jesus. His first question (18:32) is brand-new to this gospel. In John's account, it is Pilate's idea and might reflect his cynicism about Jewish leadership. Notice that Jesus is not submissive toward Pilate. Jesus puts questions to him and tells him the truth—truth which neither Pilate nor the leaders outside are able to grasp. He states his mission (18:38). Pilate's response is a sardonic dismissal.

But the reader gets it all—and that is the purpose of John's writing.

Plainly, Pilate doesn't understand why Jesus has been brought to him, so he tries unsuccessfully to release Jesus instead of Barabbas.

Pilate has Jesus scourged. Scourging was usual after condemnation and before crucifixion. No reason is given here for the altered timing; perhaps Pilate was aiming for a lesser torture than crucifixion for Jesus. The soldiers scourge and mock Jesus with a terrible crown and a robe worn only by royalty—all a bitter play on the charge later to be recorded against Jesus: King of the Jews. Then Pilate brings Jesus outside to show the leaders that he has already punished Jesus. But rather than satisfying them, the sight of Jesus incenses them the more.

When Pilate argues momentarily for Jesus' innocence, the leaders shout their real objection to Jesus. Jesus is not eager to respond to Pilate's further inquiries and affirms that the whole event is not under Pilate's control. Pilate's next attempt to free Jesus is repudiated by the Jewish leaders' implication of Pilate's disloyalty to Rome. The situation is too tight for Pilate.

An interesting twist occurs in 19:13. Scholars do not agree about the translation of *seated*. The grammatical form of the Greek verb can mean either that Pilate sat down (the normal procedure for judgment) or that Pilate had Jesus sit down on the judge's bench. If Jesus is seated on the bench, then who is on trial? To whom have the leaders unwittingly submitted their case?

Pilate's last sarcastic question completes the rejection of Jesus, and Pilate orders crucifixion.

For Your Reflection

Reexamine the whole scene, looking closely at all of Jesus'

replies. If these statements provided all the information you had about Jesus, what would you know about him?

Now look through the scene again. Find all the titles applied to Jesus, no matter who says them. Recall that one of John's habits is to present the truth (ironic and often misunderstood) in other mouths than Jesus' own.

Which moment in this scene interests you the most? Place yourself within it. Come as close to its events as you can. Pray within these events as your heart prompts you.

The main thrust of the Pilate scene is Jesus. Can we learn something from him for our own lives?

The overwhelming impression of Jesus in this scene is of a majestic poise. He is not defensive, he is truthful; he pauses when he does not wish to reply, he does not protest. He simply does not yield to the insanity around him, neither to Roman power nor to violent accusers.

How did he become so poised? He knew who he was. He knew that, appearances to the contrary, he was not victimized by the powerful people around him. He knew that all was in perfect accord with the will of his beloved Father—the only desire Jesus had. His sense of identity was simply not connected to these events; his personhood was established firmly in God.

He shows us what is possible in God. The more our own identity moves away from our petty concerns toward an increasing devotion to the Lord, the less reason we have to be defensive or frightened or even affected by unwanted events.

No doubt when you ponder your own poise-in-God, you will see—as I do—that you have a long way to go. But our direction is pointed out to us by Jesus' response to Pilate.

What aspect of your life might provide you with a chance to practice Jesus' majestic attitude? Almost any area involving authority or the personal power of others might do. If you find Jesus' poise attractive, discuss it with him. Ask for guidance about how you might practice in your own challenging situation. Then when an idea comes to you, be sure to carry it out, both as an experiment and as an offering to the Lord. You may be quite surprised at the result!

Jesus' Crucifixion and Death

At the beginning of the story of the crucifixion (19:16b-37), John notes that Jesus carried his cross "by himself." With these words, John asserts again that Jesus is in full control.

The inscription, written as a criminal charge but proclaiming the truth in all languages used in Jerusalem, announces Jesus' real inner identity. And, incidentally, Pilate gets in his last word in his ongoing quarrel with Jewish leaders.

With the authors of the Synoptics—but in a quite different way—John refers to Psalm 22, especially verse 19. But here it is no cry of distress. Scripture is fulfilled by the soldiers' actions, just as in other Johannine scenes someone besides Jesus fulfills the Old Testament.

Why does John so emphasize Jesus' seamless tunic, which even the soldiers did not split? Opinions vary, so no solid proof is possible. Here is one possibility to ponder: a seamless garment is of *one* piece, not divided. It may thus symbolize the unity John's Jesus so often evokes: unity between Jesus and the Father, unity between Jesus and the disciples. If so, it is a unity that even the forces of darkness (symbolized by the cold indifference of the soldiers) do not divide.

If John did intend something like this, how reassuring it can be to us. Our aim for unity with the Father and with Jesus will not be destroyed by the opposition and divisions of life. We need only keep our own heart focused on God—and though we may suffer, the union we desire cannot be thwarted by external forces, no matter how powerful.

The next moment of the passion is familiar and beloved. By Jesus' cross stand three or four women, including Jesus' mother, and the "disciple whom he loved." Mother and disciple are given to each other. On the literal level, Jesus has fulfilled his obligations as the son of a widow by providing for her care. Much more is suggested in this scene, however.

We do not *know* the identity of the "beloved disciple." Devotional tradition suggests that it was John the Apostle, but he is never identified as such in Scripture. Unidentified, he can symbolize all equally beloved disciples, including—perhaps especially—the reader of this gospel. John emphasizes discipleship throughout. Many have pointed out that in John, Mary, Jesus' mother, is treated more as a disciple than as his personal mother. So it may be that this loving act of the dying Lord is about discipleship. If so, it begs for reflection. (See For Your Reflection on page 79.)

Then, in 19:28-30, where we read of his death, Jesus is still actively in charge. He knows that he has completed his task. In the words "I thirst," some see a summation of the whole of John's gospel and of Jesus' whole mission. For what does Jesus thirst? Surely not the wine! He thirsts for the Father and the Father's will (in John 4:34, God's will is Jesus' food); he thirsts for his own, his disciples, for unity of heart with each one of them. He longs, as the Last Discourses repeatedly show, for all to be one in himself and thus one with the Father.

He takes the wine as a symbol, too, for it is placed on a sprig of hyssop, which would not actually support the weight of a sponge. Hyssop was used in the Passover ritual, a reminder of the mark of the blood of the lamb that preserved the Israelites from the angel of death in the story of the Exodus from Egypt

(Exodus 12:22-23). Does hyssop here intimate that those who follow this crucified Jesus will also not know death?

Jesus declares, then, that he has completed the work of the Father, that he has given his whole life for his friends to empower them to come to the Father in him. So he actively and deliberately "hands over his spirit." To the end, all power belongs to Jesus. And maybe his "handing over" is not only a dying but a releasing of the Holy Spirit for its work in the world (as some scholars assert).

Remaining is the strong symbol of the lancing of Jesus' side. Jesus was dead abnormally soon, so his bones were left intact—as required by Old Testament law for the paschal lamb of sacrifice. Yet a soldier (once again a fulfiller of Scripture) lanced his side, releasing both water and blood—highly symbolic, highly significant, since John insists that this was witnessed.

Water is generally understood to symbolize the Spirit, given through baptismal water. It is life and power to the body and especially life and power for the human spirit in its journey toward indwelling in Christ Jesus. For just as the Spirit abides in the believer's heart, so the Spirit came to the believers through Jesus' dying.

The blood of Jesus is the blood given for the life of the world, and it is the blood of the Eucharist as well (portended in John 6). Another symbolic meaning for this blood, one that though not often encountered is a traditional one nevertheless. Blood symbolizes not only life but the innermost wisdom of the heart; for the ancients, the heart was the source of the blood *and* the innermost "place" where God could be known.

Isn't it from Jesus' heart that our own experience of God is enabled? Isn't it through Jesus' death, and the giving of his own blood, that we increasingly participate in the divine life?

And doesn't our participation in his life give us spiritual wisdom?

For Your Reflection

If Jesus' giving of his mother/disciple to the "beloved disciple" and him to her is about discipleship, what can we learn from it?

At the very least, we learn that disciples are mutually responsible to take care of one another. This quality may be seriously lacking in today's churches. It is so easy to care for friends who happen to be in the parish but so difficult sometimes to take care of others simply because they are Jesus' disciples, too—or like ourselves, trying to become good disciples. Too often we focus on whether we like one another's personality instead of on the devotion and faith we share and what it calls us to become.

I doubt that Jesus' mother and the Beloved Disciple, in the moment of Jesus' dying, were thinking about whether or not they liked each other. They were totally focused on Jesus. The key for us, too, is that if our whole focus is on the Lord, we can and will care for one another.

Consider your own relationships with other Christians, especially those in your own parish. Do you divide yourself from them? Are you open-hearted to all? Is there a "most difficult parishioner" whom you reject?

If you find divisions in your heart, in your prayer stand at Jesus' cross with that disliked person (or persons) and hear Jesus give you to each other. Will you accept? How will you express your new understanding? We have seen this point made three times now in the passion of John, each with a different nuance. Do you get the feeling that Jesus wanted something of us?

In dying, Jesus released the Spirit of God into the world in a new way. Especially, he released the Spirit into the hearts of his disciples. (See also John 20:22.) In the Last Discourses, Jesus had said, "It is better for you that I go. For if I do not go, the Advocate will not come to you. But if I go, I will send him to you" (John 16:7). Now Jesus has given his disciples this supreme gift: the Spirit of God to live in our heart.

It is important to know that this is not an abstraction. Often, because at confirmation we experienced nothing in particular, we think the Spirit is an abstract concept, distant from our experience of life. The reasons for this misunderstanding are many, but what we can do about it is simple: open our heart. Ask Jesus to help us know the Spirit directly. Ask the Spirit to express itself through us.

Don't pray such a prayer unless you really want it, though, because it is sure to be answered yes, and your life will change forever. But no change could be more adventuresome, more joyful, more fulfilling, more *real* and lasting. For it is this great gift of Spirit by which Jesus effects our union with himself and the Father. Union is not a concept; it is an experience that can become steady and constant. It is certainly not casual and cannot happen overnight. It is the highest goal of all Christian spiritual life. It is divine love fulfilling itself.

Read again those passages about oneness and about love in the Last Discourses. Ponder seriously: do you want to learn to live like that? If you do, then the dying gift of Jesus, the Spirit itself, is for you. Ask—and your new life, your own rebirth or transformation, will begin.

Jesus' Burial

Most notable in John 19:38-42 is the sheer quantity of spices used in preparing the body of Jesus for burial. Equivalent to about seventy pounds in modern weight, such an amount is staggering. Think of how much the spices in your cupboard weigh—two ounces a bottle, at most. Not only is the quantity much more than would normally be used at a burial, it represents a phenomenal expense for Nicodemus. It is a tribute of royal proportions—which is exactly John's intention. Jesus is indeed King, and he is buried as befits his true status.

For Your Reflection

Often, our familiarity with Jesus and his various titles deflects an attitude of heart that we need: honor to royalty, honor to divinity, honor to the King and the Son of God.

Many people in the West experience no analogy to such exalted position. Americans even call the holder of the highest office in the land "Mister President." It may be difficult, therefore, to catch the intensity of honor due an earthly king and even harder to capture the reverence due a heavenly King, a divine Son.

We can begin to develop honor by doing what Joseph and Nicodemus did: honor Jesus by a physical expression. What you choose to do to express your worship is not as important as choosing *something* and doing it. It may be as simple as laying a flower before the tabernacle or as complex as offering prayers accompanied by bodily gestures (like genuflection and prostration). Put up a picture of Jesus, light a candle, or put a flower there; lay some dollar bills there—whatever symbolizes for you a new level of honor to him. You may wish to remember that a self-invented act often includes more of ourselves than a recital of someone else's devotions. Be sure, however, that you involve your heart's honest reverence for Jesus. Without that, any act is empty.

If you are using this book during Lent, you may wish to

design a personal act of reverence for Good Friday, alone or with others. But at any time, you can honor Jesus' indescribable self-giving through his dying. Honor, gratitude, and undying love are our only fully appropriate responses.

CHAPTER FOUR

Putting It All Together

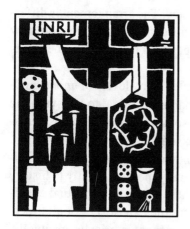

In Luke 9:23, Jesus "said to all, 'If anyone wishes to come after me, he must deny himself and take up his cross daily and follow me.'" The parallel passages in Matthew (16:24) and Mark (8:34) are the same, except that by adding "daily" Luke emphasized continuing discipleship.

This remembered statement of Jesus must have been well known in the early Christian communities. Why else would it appear in all three gospels? It must have been important to the early Christian understanding of discipleship. Because it mentions the cross, we are reminded of the passion and death of Jesus. As we have already seen, the passion offers a number of insights about discipleship as well as profound understanding of Jesus' own purpose and meaning. Let's carry our insights further.

Luke 9:23 has three elements. We will use them as a framework for deepening our understanding of the teaching about discipleship in the passion stories.

1. One must deny oneself.

2. One must take up one's cross every day.

3. One must "follow" Jesus, that is, emulate his example as well as obey his teachings.

As we look for the implications and meanings of these elements, we will include the particular insights of John's passion, even though John includes no verse similar to Luke 9:23. Some of the ideas that follow have been mentioned in earlier chapters; others will be new. The arrangement is different, though, and the new connections may give you new insights. You are invited to deepen your reflection on the points you have already encountered.

Remember that Scripture holds many levels of understanding and action, from the external or historical to the symbolic and innermost. Ultimately, the spiritual journey of transformation to which the gospels call us is an interior journey of depth. The historical or exterior journey is a beginning and an analogy. The Gospel of John, especially, points not only to history or theology (as wonderful as these are) but to spiritual conditions as well. It may be that Jesus did exteriorly, for all to see, what each of us must do (or experience) interiorly, spiritually, to bring us home to God in our own present life.

Deny Yourself

Most Christians probably think that self-denial, or denying oneself, means giving up certain foods or certain pleasures or avoiding recreation or doing something hard. It is a common notion that during Lent one is to practice self-denial at this level.

Certainly, there is nothing wrong with these practices. Compared to the deeper aspects of denying oneself, however, they are frankly child's play. They make a fine beginning for one whose orientation is still basically exterior, but they can—and eventually must—lead to other, deeper efforts.

More profound understanding of self-denial directs our efforts toward displacing the egocentric self from the center of awareness and action. It's safe to say that all of us naturally place ourselves at the center of our universe emotionally, physically, rationally, and at first, spiritually as well. But gradually, if one desires to know and to follow the Lord ever more closely, the ego gets literally "displaced" by God at the center. This self-denying process is not easy and often must be fought for, but it is essential to knowing God intimately.

Put God at the Center

The effort to displace the ego, or more accurately, to allow it to be displaced, is the flip side of the effort to put God first, to put God at the center of our universe. Actually, God already *is* at the center of our universe, but we do not recognize it because we so naturally think our own little ego-self is in that position.

To deny oneself ultimately means: God is my own center and my "me" is far out at the periphery or has disappeared altogether in total attention to the Lord. We cannot just decide to do this and—bingo!—it's done. If it were so easy, surely nothing as extreme as Jesus' crucifixion would ever have been necessary.

But we can decide that we want to move in that direction. In the end, God must do it in us, because our own action is ever subtly but powerfully ego-centered. Jesus put God first because he loved God more than anyone or anything—far more than he loved himself. Because he loved God so utterly, he wanted only to glorify God in and through his own life—and this profound desire led to his death. Jesus died, even as our ego-centered self must die, in order that God be glorified fully in us.

God displacing ego at our center is a mystery that no one has ever fully described, but many (more than we imagine) have experienced it. It is the culmination of discipleship to Jesus. It is the oneness with himself and the Father that he desired for us. Even though we cannot decide to "arrive" there suddenly, we can decide to begin and to continue the journey, which is, in an interior sense, our own passion. Such a journey is both daily effort and final.

If God is to be at the center, then our ego-centered interests, concerns, and fears must be left behind, one by one. Indeed, eventually everything that focuses on ourselves will be left behind until only God lives in our hearts. As Saint Paul put it, "I have been crucified with Christ; yet I live, no longer I, but Christ lives in me" (Galatians 2:19-20). Paul was not merely making sweet sounds here. He was describing, though incompletely, the experience of one for whom Christ is the center and whose ego-self is displaced.

If we love God and wish to be closer to him in our hearts, then the passion suggests good, practical approaches to denying ourselves more and more, to displacing our egos more and more.

Practice Obedience

In our present everyday lives, we are far from the level of obedience exemplified by Jesus. As we have seen, he obeyed the Father's slightest wish, slightest movement in his heart, because he loved the Father so totally that anything less was inconceivable. Nor can we instantly be like him. We grow in love with God and in limitation of Jesus.

Our growth is not automatic. Growth comes little by little,

but that does not mean we should relax all effort. It is good to let go of unreasonable or impossible demands on ourselves— after all, they are only another form of egocentrism. But our own effort is necessary for growth toward God to continue. We must stretch ourselves to follow the Lord.

In John 14:23-24, Jesus ties our love of him very closely to obedience to his words, which originated with the Father. We will obey to the extent that we love him, and we will love him to the extent that we obey him. It is a circle, yes, but we may step in at any point, wherever we can. Then the circle itself will carry us to greater and greater love, to deeper and deeper obedience. Thus, we will gradually learn to obey Jesus' new and highest command: to love one another as he has loved.

Caution: never try to behave as if you love that much when in fact you don't. Nothing can make you sick any faster than that. Growth in obedience to such a grand commandment requires daily honesty with ourselves and daily patience with our distance from our goal. It is possible to find the edge where we *could* obey more, love more, if we made a truthful effort.

For example, I may actually be able to give fifteen minutes more attention to loving the Lord in prayer or to expressing love to another in a note or a phone call. I may not be able to devote my whole life to others' welfare as Dorothy Day did. But if I refuse to give the little that I can, I stop my own growth toward God.

Give Up the Miseries

Watching Jesus during the passion, we are struck again and again with the quality of his responses to the taunts and tortures he undergoes. Such majesty is possible because Jesus' human ego has departed and only his union with the Father remains.

Our greatest ego-indulgence is not usually in pleasures or

even in acquisitions. We indulge our egocentrism most solidly when we focus on the negative in our thoughts or our words or our actions. As my psychologist brother, Dr. Lloyd Thomas, neatly puts it: we B-CAD. According to him, B-CAD means "bitch, complain, accuse, defend." These are tremendous ego trips. We do not find Jesus doing such things during the passion. When we even think of Jesus like that, it is obvious how far from discipleship B-CADding is.

Yet Jesus had plenty of opportunity to do every one of those things, didn't he? Quickly review the passion events in your memory. Almost every one could have been an invitation to B-CAD, but Jesus simply did not resist what happened to him. We can, with sustained practice, learn to do the same, for love of him.

We B-CAD far more than we realize until we begin to look deliberately at how we are. We may or may not act out our negative impulses, but we do speak them and we do think them. Nothing solidifies our egocentrism more than this nearly constant flow of B-CADding. It pushes us away from the Lord; it makes love nearly impossible; it hides from us the joy and beauty that Jesus wants us to experience.

No area of our life is immune to B-CADding. Examine your own habits. Then you can begin intelligently to reduce the B-CADding in your life. Every time you see it, you can simply stop it. As it disappears, love will appear more and more, and you will begin to live in Jesus' words as he desires. Then Jesus' promise in John 14:23 will begin to be fulfilled for you.

Not B-CADding, in imitation of Jesus' passion, includes not trying to prove ourselves right, even when our reputation is at stake. There is a wonderful story about Saint Gerard Majella, C.SS.R. His monastery was in a village, and one day a village women came to see his superior. She said her daughter was pregnant by Brother Gerard. The superior went to Brother Gerard and scolded him bitterly, giving him a severe penance and making the accusation known in the community. Brother Gerard lived under that painful penance and community disgrace.

Then after many months, the woman came again, this time to tell the superior that the girl had admitted that the father of her baby was a young man in the village. The superior called Brother Gerard in and demanded to know why he had not denied paternity in the beginning. Brother Gerard said simply, "You did not ask me." Would you say that Brother Gerard denied himself? What do you think happened to his ego in the meantime?

Closely related to freedom from self-defensiveness is the ability to ignore mockery, blame, or other verbal maltreatment. Experiences such as ridicule and derision upset and frighten us if we do not know with certitude who we are and what our life purpose is. Those who have said a serious yes to discipleship need not be upset, because they know their main desire in life: to be disciples of Jesus.

When one deeply knows that "I am going to God no matter what," then lots of energy is available for growing discipleship *regardless of other people's actions.* We may feel fine about ourselves or we may not; but if we are going to God, we are less concerned about self-esteem. We may know that others like us or scorn us, but we walk calmly beyond both because we are going to God. We may recognize that we experience ego-related pain as we move beyond circumstances, but we keep going because that kind of pain signals profound inner healing in progress.

Gradually, the one who seeks God more than anything else discovers that nothing matters except what can be used for coming closer to the Lord. Derision or blame or similar experiences, when not resisted, displace the ego and leave space for the love of the Lord to grow.

Once a friend of mine had to endure public reproach from one she loved very much. She is a person who longs for full relationship with God. So she stood and took the reproach, all the while aware that God's love included both her and the person who was making the trouble. She offered no resistance to the experience. A few days later, when the sting of it had subsided, she became aware that her prayer was much deeper and more still than it had ever been. In her inner silence, God was vividly present.

Do you think there was a connection between her self-denial and her deepened prayer? If Jesus had spent precious energy resisting and defending himself, do you think he would have been able to maintain his unity with the Father as we have seen especially in John's gospel?

Remorse and Forgiveness

If we are blessed with remorse as Peter was, and if we let it burn away our wrongs instead of resisting it and merely feeling guilty, we will experience a deeper level of self-denial, of ego-displacement. In remorse, we recognize our inability to raise ourselves by our own bootstraps. Then we can pray with Teresa of Avila, "Lord, I will never be any better unless you make me so." That gives God more space within us to act. Intensity and cleanness of remorse lead us naturally to seek forgiveness. Half-conscious guilt, kept and hidden, just pushes us deeper into our false ego-sufficiency. Remorse is so painful and so inescapable that we only want to be made right again. So we beg the Lord to forgive us.

Whenever we need to ask forgiveness, we must do it, even

though we may also feel we are not worthy of forgiveness. This is, perhaps, a difference between Peter and Judas. Judas maintained his ego-sufficiency, even at the cost of his own death and separation from the Lord. Peter's remorse displaced much of his ego. So he could accept the Lord's forgiveness and become the great apostle he became.

We should never harm ourselves, even mentally, for *any* wrongdoing. We are invited to live in a constant stream of forgiveness if we need it. If we have done something (in thought, word, or action) that is less than we want to be, then we must take it to the Lord for forgiveness. As we saw with the thief beside Jesus on Golgotha, Jesus withholds nothing when the penitent desires him. We can trust that.

On the other hand, thinking we don't deserve forgiveness is also an egocentric stance. It displaces the ego to *know* that we don't deserve forgiveness and yet to still accept it as the gracious gift of a loving Lord.

Being Whoever We Are

In Luke 22:24-27, we saw that the disciples, even at the Last Supper, were interested in who was better, greater than the others. Jesus told them that they completely misunderstood. Interest in more status, more position, more power than we have is not part of discipleship. Letting go of such interests is part of self-denial.

Perhaps most of us have no interest anyway in being at the top of the status ladder like, say, the president of the United States or even the top person in the company. Many of us are not especially ambitious for wide fame. For us, denying ourselves by letting go of interest in "who's better" means letting go of comparing ourselves to others in any way at all. We can practice stopping every time we notice that we are comparing ourselves to our friends or coworkers, to others in our club or our parish—or even to saints. It doesn't matter with whom we are comparing ourselves. It is the comparing itself that is ego-centered: Who is better than *me*? Who is worse than *me*?

To let go of interest in who is better, Jesus suggested the practice of serving all others. This does not mean one should not accept leadership and responsibility. Leaders sometimes serve completely. But disciples do not seek leadership for its own sake or for its by-products, such as respect from others or social status.

Be concerned to deny yourself by humble service, as Jesus recommended. Then you will not need to compare yourself to others, because you will be denying your ego-interests in favor of love and humility. You won't even have to think about whether you are loving or humble. Those virtues will come of themselves when you serve without self-comparisons for the Lord.

All these suggestions, drawn from the example and words of the Lord during his passion, are powerful practices for denying oneself. The next step in our guiding quotation is "take up your cross daily."

Take Up Your Cross Daily

What is your own cross? I used to think it had to be a smaller version of Jesus' cross: a self-sacrifice for others' redemption. More recently, I have come to think that *any* challenge can be a cross if we use it to bring ourselves closer to the Lord and if we offer it to him for redemptive purposes. Attitude can transform any challenge into a cross with power to bring us closer to God's heart—a lesser version of the power that Jesus' cross had.

Some people experience huge, even tragic, challenges in

life. Catastrophic events do happen. But the gigantic challenges are almost never "daily," as Luke mentioned.

Other people seldom go through major life-changing events. Almost everyone experiences the death of loved ones, but that is normal in life, however painful. Few of us encounter any emergency as enormous as crucifixion.

All disciples are called to take up their cross, little or gigantic. Many people accept large challenges, big pains, violent emergencies, with great resourcefulness and courage. They survey what has happened, what is required, and march forward with determination and sometimes with love and gratitude.

Yet these same people may not do well at all with the daily "nastiness" in their ordinary lives. As a postcard I once saw put it: "I'm very good at emergencies and totally unprepared for everyday life." Of course, the reverse is true for many people. At daily life they are creative, steady, and wise, but they collapse in an emergency.

The point here is that a cross can be a daily matter as well as a crisis event. Our native ability to deal with one or the other will vary, but as disciples we are called to learn to carry whatever challenge each day brings.

Assume Some Tough Times

One of the most dangerous assumptions for modern disciples is the assumption that life "should be" all ease, comfort, and sweetness. No life is. The view of life-without-difficulty promoted by the media is simply erroneous. Such a view is dangerous for spiritual life because it makes our real life seem somehow wrong. Either *we* are wrong to have difficulties or we've been given a bad deal by life or we feel called upon to force our daily life to be trouble-free.

Disciples know—or are learning—that troubles enter life for a reason: to help us grow closer to God. They will accomplish their purpose in us *if* we "take up our cross daily," if we accept the challenges as opportunities to live beyond them, rooted in our love for God.

One of my long-held notions about asceticism is that few of us need to give ourselves *more* discomfort than life already gives us. As disciples, we do learn to accept and shoulder the unsought events that life sends our way. And we try never to waste them by resisting them. Instead, we can practice quietly saying to ourselves, *This is what God wants me to experience right now. It will pass. How can I learn its lesson before it vanishes?* Accepting the troubles in our life consciously and without resentment is one way of taking up our daily cross.

Focus on Love

When we read John's gospel closely enough, we see that Jesus is not reluctant about his coming troubles. He anticipates his "hour" when he can fully accomplish the Father's wishes, not with dread but with a readiness, like that of a runner poised at the starting line. He or she knows the race will be long but is ready and willing to take off.

Jesus' readiness was based on his profound unquestioning love for the Father and his total confidence in the Father's intentions. When we take up our own daily difficulties, they will fulfill in us their redemptive potential if we focus on our love for the Lord; our troubles will become, like Jesus' cross, the means by which we grow deeper into God.

Knowing that these events are rooted in love, we will recognize that they are tailor-made for us by the divine Tailor. Just as Jesus' work on the cross was designed for him by the Father of love, so are our troubles fitted precisely to our needs.

In the beginning of our conscious efforts, we may not recognize that wonderful truth. But if we use our hindsight a few times, we see that every trouble, well lived and not wasted, leaves us with a lesson learned, a stage of growth completed, a stronger awareness of God in our lives. That is exactly what crosses, taken daily, do for us.

Do You Need Help?

Some people, like John's Jesus, carry their crosses by themselves. (See John 19:17.) Other people need and receive help just as Jesus in the Synoptics accepted help from Simon, the Cyrenian. About this there is really only one thing to say: if you need help to carry your daily cross well, with courage and strength, by all means get that help. If this means counseling, get it. If it means talking to a friend, do it. If it means asking other people to give you a hand, ask.

Practically all of us do need God's help to carry our crosses, so all of us pray for the Lord's assistance. It may come in any form—in our own resources or through the help of other people. Nowhere are we told that we have to carry our cross by ourselves. So unless we are sure we can, let's seek out any help we need.

Take Responsibility

Sometimes our biggest cross is ourselves. Especially if we have had a traumatic past, we may have big problems with ourselves. The key to taking up this daily (and nightly!) cross is accepting our own responsibility for who we are.

This does *not* imply that we are somehow at fault for being this way or that we should feel guilty for what others have contributed to our struggles. It means, rather, that we take a clear look at the way we are and shoulder the possibility of helping ourselves be better, freer, kinder, happier. We carry ourselves, like a crossbeam, with acceptance even of the pain until our next step is completed.

Saint Therese, the Little Flower, said that if you can be contented amid your own weaknesses, you will make of your heart a pleasant garden for the Lord to dwell in. That suggests doing what you can to keep the weeds down but not fretting about what is still left at the end of a day.

So if your hardest cross is yourself, be like Jesus: carry it bravely, and don't worry too much about how you got to be the way you are. Do what you can, and leave the rest up to the Lord; he will gladly be your Simon.

Waking Up

The disciples slept in Gethsemane even though Jesus had told them to stay awake and pray. Waking up, when it is so comfortable to sleep, can be as challenging as any cross.

When we'd rather not see our weaknesses, we go to sleep. When we'd rather not commit ourselves to discipleship, we go to sleep. When we choose physical sleep over morning prayer or other practices, we are asleep spiritually as well. If we close our eyes to others' needs when we can do something about them, we choose sleep.

The wide-awake person *sees* what life really is like and also sees the Lord in all of it. Being awake is being fully conscious of what is going on inside oneself as well as around oneself. Waking up means being totally aware of what is happening in *this* present moment. Being awake means, as Jesus suggested and did, taking all circumstances to prayer.

Waking up is not easy. In fact, it takes most people a lifetime to become fully awake, and many don't even know it is desirable. Nevertheless, Jesus wanted his disciples to be alert and aware—of themselves, of life, and most of all, awake to himself in love.

Daily cross-carrying means daily effort to wake up and discover the reality of the Lord's presence and action in every moment of every day and to acknowledge him with gratitude and love, no matter what else the day contains.

Stay With It

Cross-carrying was, even for Jesus, a matter of putting one foot ahead of the other until he got where he was going. It is a figure for us: keep going.

Discipleship is not completed in a week. The cross is not carried to its fulfillment in a single surge of effort. That's why Luke says discipleship is daily. So we know when we take up our cross today that we also expect to take it up tomorrow and tomorrow, for as long as it takes.

Don't expect quick, obvious results from your efforts to take up your daily-cross opportunities. Notice gratefully the little lights, the little steps, the little encouragements. Say thanks to the Lord—and keep walking. Eventually, cross-carrying becomes a habit and supports us with familiarity. Then we may be free, as Jesus was free: to take the initiative, to stay in charge inwardly, and in the end to hand over our completed tasks with joy to the Father.

"...And Follow Me"

The third portion of our verse says that having denied ourselves (displaced our ego from center) and taken up our cross, we are invited to follow Jesus. Of course, we do not have to complete one, then turn to the next. They grow simultaneously in us and reinforce each other.

In following Jesus, we take him as our example and we heed

his teaching afresh; here, of course, in the passion. Jesus is a *large* example in the passion, nearly overwhelming. So we have considered the passion's elements one by one. For immediate help, however, we can practice its principles in incomplete ways; they will not remain incomplete forever.

For practice, you may wish to choose just three of the following suggestions to explore in reflection and in action. Then be sure to follow through on them.

Take Refuge in God's Love

As we have seen repeatedly, Jesus relied with total confidence on the love of the Father. Jesus knew, first of all, that the Father *is* love itself and that there is no lesser nature in him. But Jesus seems to have further taken this knowledge quite personally when he says the Father loves *him* because he obeys the Father's wishes. (See John 5:19-20.) For Jesus, the Father's love was everything.

For us, the love of the Lord is probably important but not yet everything. So we can practice increasing its importance by trusting God's love for more and more of our life. One of the best practices, always available, is to accept the unpleasant as Jesus accepted his passion, that is, as coming from the loving hand of the Lord, trusting that it *is* a loving gift and treating it accordingly.

Seek Oneness With the Lord

As portrayed in John, Jesus experienced his life, his suffering, and his death in unbroken union with God. He wanted to give the same union to his disciples. But the Lord rarely gives good gifts before the disciple wants them or is ready to receive them.

To follow Jesus we begin by consciously desiring to be

united with Jesus, with God, in unbroken union. This is the largest and truest desire a human being can cherish. It is the most challenging and the most rewarding that human life can offer. It is the purpose of human life and of Christian faith. At the very least, the magnificent possibility of union with God deserves an honest response. Do we want it? Are we interested in it?

When people tell themselves the truth, their responses vary. Some people really don't care so much about union with God, or at most, maybe far away in some distant, future heaven. Some people have never thought it possible, so haven't considered it. Some want union with the Lord if it doesn't cost too much in their personal life, if it is an easy-to-get experience. Some want union with God no matter what it costs and no matter how long it takes.

Whatever degree of desire for God you find in your own heart, take it to prayer and tell him the truth. If you want only a little, say so. If you want all of God, say so. If you find that you rather wish you wanted God more, then make that your prayer.

If you want God a great deal, a particularly effective prayer is to pray for the full enlivening of the Holy Spirit within your own heart, your own life. Jesus died in part so that the Holy Spirit would come into the hearts of his followers. (See John 16:7.) He wants you to have that great Spirit fully alive within you; it will unite you with him and the Father. Do you want God enough to pray for the Spirit and "go for it" as a disciple?

Obey What You Know

Since Jesus knew exactly what the Father's will was, he knew what to do. He did what he perceived the Father to be about. We, however, are not always so clear about what God wants in our lives. Even when we do our best to discern his direction, we sometimes miss.

Missing is not worth our worry, however. The Father's love will not vanish from our lives if we don't understand his guidance. It is important only to put into action what we *do* understand. For example, if you believe God wants you to spend twenty minutes every morning in prayer, it is vital that you do it. If you understand a verse of Scripture that applies to something in your life, it is vital that you act on it. What you don't know, leave for later.

Not obeying has unwanted consequences. We feel guilty and therefore trapped; we feel farther from God—the exact opposite of what we want; and we will not be given further guidance until we use the guidance we have understood.

That last consequence is perhaps the hardest of all, but it is reasonable. If you are teaching a child about science, you do not proceed to the complex until the child has understood and can explain the basics. It is the same with God and our discipleship; he will give further guidance when we have practiced what we already know. Jesus said if we are faithful in little things, larger ones will be given. (See Luke 19:17, for example.) If we obey the small guidance, further understanding will be given.

Let Jesus Be King

Over and over in the passion, Jesus is called "King of the Jews." He is accused and derided as king, he is robed as king, he is presented by Pilate as king. Yet we know that he is not a political king—not then, not now. Instead, he is a spiritual king. Most important, he will be our personal king if we allow him to be. He will rule our lives if we obey him.

Good kings are committed to the welfare of their subjects—prosperity, security, full well-being. Jesus the King is committed to all that—and more—in the lives of his disciples. The question is whether we are committed subjects of this king.

Jesus has demonstrated how to have a king: he was totally given over to the Father in love and trust and obedience. So we can imitate him and allow him to be the same kind of king in our lives as the Father was for him: totally loving and totally self-giving. Furthermore, we know Jesus is trustworthy as our king because he himself was a fully trustworthy Son of God. That is what he wants us to become and will empower us to become (John 1:12 again).

In this, as in all things that truly matter, Jesus' example goes before us as a lantern in a dark night. Let us follow it—it's all we have.

Care for One Another

Over and over during the passion reflections, we have seen the vital importance of disciples caring for one another. This point cannot be overemphasized. Jesus commanded his disciples to love one another as he loved them. It sounds overwhelming indeed, and we must not mentally punish ourselves for not yet being able to do it. But if we want to do it, the Lord will help.

What we can do, even this very minute, is express our willingness to learn to love that much and ask the Lord to teach us. We can take Jesus' new commandment more seriously than we ever have. Then we can invent some simple expressions of love for others, according to our present capacity. Our capacity will grow!

Jesus expressed his own care for all during the passion in at least three remarkable ways.

- He washed Judas' feet along with the others, thus not excluding his betrayer from his love.

- He expressed compassion and forgiveness for his torturers as well as for his sleeping, falling disciples.
- He was open to the needs of those around him, even in his own extreme pain.

The third way Jesus expressed his care can certainly be practiced almost every day. In many ways, we live with pain, either physical, emotional, or mental hurts. Too easily, we allow these to become the center of our attention, and they shut out our love for others, our interest in others, our openness to others. This is especially frequent inside the family—and especially destructive there.

In reality, we can learn to focus beyond our pain on something we love or wish to love. We already do it more often than we think. We passionately love to dance, for example, fatigue or even an injury may not prevent us from fully enjoying dancing. Or for those intensely in love with another, even troublesome emotions and thoughts can be forgotten when the two are together.

As a practice in loving the Lord, then, we can *choose* to focus on other people but beyond our own pain, as Jesus did and for his sake.

Courage! Peace! Truth!

These are big words, aren't they? We see Jesus exemplifying them throughout his passion. He faces it all with quiet courage. He does not lose his peace, especially in John's gospel. And he speaks only the truth about himself or others.

How can we practice imitating this? By beginning with small instances. Do you have to go to the dentist? Be brave by choice—yes, you can. You need not give in to fear, and you need not complain about it. There are dozens of such opportunities every day. Look for them. Use them as adventuresome practice for a day when more courage may be needed.

How do we practice peace? First, by reflecting long on Jesus' words in John 14:27. He gives his kind of peace, not like the world's peace. One difference is that Jesus' peace is interior and does not depend on circumstances. It comes from him directly to our hearts. If we ask for it and are willing to accept it, we will find in our own experience that we can be inwardly peaceful in the midst of almost any external chaos. All at once? Not likely, but pay attention to the Lord's action in your heart and remember peacefulness often.

Here's a small example. When I have to do something I inherently don't enjoy, like shopping for groceries, my husband will often remind me to "be peaceful." It's a good practice. You can find other practices that suit you even better.

We have already considered speaking the truth. This, too, is for practice. Try not to bloody the end of your tongue, but simply stop every time you notice that you are speaking anything less than the truth. Ponder often Jesus' perfect example, especially before Pilate in John.

Prepare—and Be Ready for Anything

In Luke 22:35-36, Jesus tells his disciples to prepare themselves for difficulties coming. Of course, in that context, Jesus is referring to his own passion and perhaps to later trials the early Christians would undergo. But the value of Jesus' advice is not limited to that time or situation.

Recently a friend in her mid forties went to the hospital on Friday afternoon feeling a little ill. The next Monday morning, she died. All of us have witnessed or experienced events that radically altered someone's life. Seeing such events, we must recognize that *there are no guarantees*. Everything changes. Nothing stays the same always, except the love of the Lord.

That recognition alone will prepare us pretty deeply for the unexpected or the difficult. It is good to ponder the radical unpredictability of our life. We need not let it frighten us. It is just a universal fact that honest acknowledgment will help us accept when we need extra strength.

If we know there are no guarantees except the love of God, then where might we wish to put our main energies and attention? What—or whom—can we truly count on through everything else?

Every bit of ourselves and our resources that we invest in God will be held in absolute trust for us, to be returned in the best possible way and the best possible time. Love of God alone is genuine preparation for anything that may happen. If we root ourselves in Jesus, if we allow him to become truly the vine to which we are attached as a branch (see John 15:1-6), then we will stand firm, even if we are momentarily shaken.

One powerful practice to help root us in Jesus is regular, attentive participation in the Eucharist. When I was a brand-new Catholic (yesterday, as I write, was my twentieth anniversary), I remember feeling the wonder of always having the Eucharist available. In times of pain, in times of celebration, in times of puzzlement, in times of delight, in death, and in daily life, the Eucharist was there to steady me, to remind me of what I was most truly about, to root me a little bit more solidly in God. I recommend, without reservation, participation in Eucharist as often as you possibly can.

Another powerful practice for rooting ourselves in God is to pray to God about everything, little and big, easy and hard, begging or praising. Whatever we bring to him, we do it as an offering, ready to relinquish our will to his larger, more loving will. That's what Jesus did in Gethsemane. We try to follow his example. The more we leave in God's hands, the more God occupies our own center. We look less and less to ourselves for what we hope for and more and more to God. Gradually, we recognize that it is God himself that we long for most and that all the little petitions have focused us on God alone. That is really the purpose of prayer like Jesus' prayer.

Expect Joy

In John 15:11, Jesus says, "I have told you this so that my joy might be in you and your joy might be complete." I take "told you this" to refer to all of Jesus' teachings as well as his predictions of the passion. His purpose in all he gave and all he suffered was to give us joy. Does that amaze you? It always seems amazing to me. But isn't it grand?

We humans are often a little strange about joy. It is almost as if we don't quite trust it, or we think it's "too good to be real." Some of us, when joy touches our hearts, think something must be wrong.

So practice with joy is essential if we are to be able to receive what Jesus wants us to experience: joy like his inner joy. He offers it and offers it. To receive it, we want to be fully willing to accept it and to cherish it when we notice its presence in our heart.

We can practice simply by deliberately focusing on the slightest stirring of joy, then cherishing it and taking inner care of it, en*joy*ing it. And, of course, we give thanks for joy whenever it arises. It is always a loving gift from our Lord.

Finally...

Let's remember that the passion was not the end of the whole story. Let's develop faith in God's power and will to bring beauty out of everything we go through. The Lord loves to bring ever-deeper life out of every little death.

Our own version of Jesus' passion will not be as momentous or as challenging as his was. But resurrection as a principle applies to every small death, every little interior self-denial, every trouble well lived, every small way we follow the Lord. In the passion of our own life, the cross we take up daily becomes itself our strength. Resurrection inevitably follows, by the power and the love of God. Let's remember this, every hour of every day. It is the most marvelous truth of our discipleship.

Jesus said he would not leave us orphans (see John 14:18) but would be with us. If the Lord is with us and if resurrection joy is his promise to his disciples, then how can we do any less but love him with all of our being? Why would we want to do less? In that loving is everything we have ever desired or imagined—and infinitely more, because Jesus loved the Father and us enough to pass through his own passion to his own resurrection.

God offers it all to us. How shall we respond?

Appendix

The easiest and best way to compare the passion stories in the four gospels is to photocopy all of them. Then lay the copies side by side, matching sections so you can easily see what is the same and what is different. If you do not want to do that or do not have access to a photocopier, however, you may refer to the following list of references for comparison. The questions and comments that follow each set of references tell what to look for in all the gospels.

The Agony in the Garden

Matthew 26:36-46; Mark 14:32-42; Luke 22:39-46

(Notice that John has no account of the agony in the garden.)

- What does Jesus tell the disciples to pray for?
- What are Jesus' own experiences in the garden?
- In which gospel do we read about the angel and the blood like sweat?
- How many times does Jesus return to his disciples?

Betrayal and Arrest

Matthew 26:47-56; Mark 14:43-52;
Luke 22:47-53; John 18:1-11

- Where does the kiss of betrayal actually happen?
- What happens when the servant's ear is cut off? Who does that?
- Who is in charge of the action in each gospel? Is it stronger in one gospel than in the others?
- What kind of dialogue does Jesus have with his captors?
- Compare the last two verses of this section in each gospel. What other details vary?

The Sanhedrin

Matthew 26:57-68; Mark 14:53-65; Luke 22:66-71 (John has no Sanhedrin meeting but mentions Annas in 18:12-14,19-24.)

Notice the difference in order: Peter's denial precedes the Sanhedrin in Luke and is interspersed with the Annas scenes in John.

- What does Jesus say in each scene? When is he silent? Where is he strongest?
- What are the charges against Jesus?
- What words of Jesus climax the scene?
- Which gospel omits mockery?
- In which gospel does Jesus appear not to be on trial? Why?
- Look for other differences in detail.

Peter's Denial

Matthew 26:69-75; Mark 14:66-72; Luke 22:54-62;
John 18:15-18, 25-27

- Are there differences in the intensity of Peter's reactions to the questions about Jesus?
- Which gospel has the charcoal fire? Which gospels have no fire at all?
- Compare the cockcrows and other details about Peter's denial.
- Does Peter seem different in John? How?

Jesus Before Pilate

Matthew 27:1-2, 11-31; Mark 15:1-20; Luke 23:1-25; John 18:28-40, 19:1-16

- What does Jesus say to Pilate in each gospel? Where is he silent?
- What does Pilate's wife have to do with the hearing?
- What is Herod's role, and in which gospel does he appear?
- Where is the story of Barabbas found? Are the gospels alike?
- What are the charges against Jesus when he is before Pilate?
- Are they the same as before the Sanhedrin?
- Which gospels have mockery scenes? Are they in the same place?
- Where is the scourging of Jesus mentioned? What is its motive?
- Compare the actions of the crowd in each gospel.
- How would you describe Jesus generally in Luke? in John?

Way of the Cross

Matthew 27:32; Mark 15:21; Luke 23:26-31;
John 19:16b-17

These are easily compared. Notice especially from which gospels the traditional Stations of the Cross are drawn. Notice the big difference in John's Gospel.

The Crucifixion

Matthew 27:33-44; Mark 15:22-32; Luke 23:33-43;
John 19:17b-29

- Which aspects of the crucifixion account are unique to Luke?
- Which are unique to John?
- Compare the mocking in Matthew and in Mark.
- Where do the women appear?
- Read quickly through this section in Mark. Do the same with John. What differences in feeling or tone do you experience?
- What is the role of Pilate in each section? Why the difference?

The Death of Jesus

Matthew 27:45-56; Mark 15:33-41; Luke 23:44-49;
John 19:30-37

- Find the unique points in each gospel.
- Compare the place, identity, and role of the women in each gospel.

- What cosmic events happen in each gospel? Which had none?
- What are the main expressions of faith or recognition in each?
- Compare Jesus' actual dying as each gospel describes.

The Burial Scene

Mathew 27:57-66; Mark 15:42-47; Luke 23:50-56; John 19:38-42

- Compare the role of the women in all four gospels.
- Where do the guards appear?
- Where does Nicodemus appear?
- What elements of the scene are unique to Mark?
- How is the actual burial enriched in John?

More From Marilyn Gustin...

How to Read and Pray the Christmas Story
By examining the characters, symbols, and associations in Scripture, and discovering each gospel writer's intentions, this book offers readers a way to deepen their relationship with Christ through the Christmas story. *$3.95*

How to Read and Pray the Gospels
Blending solid biblical scholarship with a joyous faith, this booklet is the perfect guide to the gospels for all Christians. *$3.95*

How to Read and Pray the Parables
This booklet emphasizes the inner meaning of Jesus' parables to help readers gain a spiritual perspective. *$2.50*

Witness to the Light
Discovering the Spirit of John's Gospel
Invites readers to reflect upon John's Gospel in order to facilitate their own personal spiritual transformation. $4.95

You *Can* Know God
Christian Spirituality for Daily Living
This book is written for anyone who is homesick for God. Every idea and every practice in it is a readiness exercise, because readers can experience God right where they are and know the Lord more and more directly in their ordinary lives. *$9.95*

Order from your local bookstore or write to
Liguori Publications
Box 060
Liguori, MO 63057-9999
(Please add $1.00 for postage and handling to orders under $5.00;
$1.50 to orders between $5.00 and $14.99; and $2.00 to orders over $15.00.)